LEONARD BASKIN

LEONARD BASKIN
BOWDOIN COLLEGE
MUSEUM OF ART

MCMLXII

ACKNOWLEDGEMENTS. This is the first full-scale exhibition of the work of a major contemporary American artist to be held in the seventy-year history of the Bowdoin College Museum of Art. It has been made possible mainly through income from the recent bequest of Mr. and Mrs. George Otis Hamlin. ❧ Many people have helped in a number of important ways to make this exhibition possible. Thanks are due the Boris Mirski Gallery of Boston, and particularly Mr. Alan Fink of that Gallery, for generous assistance; and the Grace Borgenicht Gallery of New York, where Mr. Richard Sisson's tireless cooperation was so indispensable that I am not sure what I would have done without it. ❧ I am indebted to Mr. William S. Lieberman, Curator of Prints and Drawings of The Museum of Modern Art, both for his many helpful suggestions and for making available to me material that I would not have been able to see otherwise. I am extremely grateful to Mr. Harold Hugo of The Meriden Gravure Company for the benefit of his invaluable counsel during the preparation of this catalogue for the press. ❧ For his sympathetic interest and encouragement during the long and often trying preparations for this exhibition, I should like to thank Professor Philip C. Beam, Director of this Museum. Carl N. Schmalz, Jr., formerly Associate Director of this Museum and now Associate Professor of Fine Arts at Amherst College, who first dreamed of this exhibition with me, provided much valued advice, particularly during the early stages of planning the exhibition. I also should like to thank my former secretary, Mrs. Sally Field, who handled both a vast and complicated correspondence and her temperamental boss with great efficiency and unfailing good humor. ❧ No words are adequate to express my deep appreciation to Winslow Ames, Julius S. Held, Harold Joachim, Rico Lebrun, and Ray Nash, who have so generously contributed the essays to this catalogue. ❧ Finally, I should like to acknowledge the generosity of the more than fifty lenders to this exhibition, especially those who have been without their works for the better part of a year, during 1961–62, while an exhibition of Baskin's work, organized by the International Council of The Museum of Modern Art, traveled to several European countries.

MARVIN S. SADIK,
Curator

LENDERS TO THE EXHIBITION

MR. AND MRS. WINSLOW AMES, SAUNDERSTOWN, RHODE ISLAND

MRS. LEONARD BASKIN, NORTHAMPTON, MASSACHUSETTS

MR. LEONARD BASKIN, NORTHAMPTON, MASSACHUSETTS

RABBI AND MRS. SAMUEL BASKIN, NEW YORK

MR. LAWRENCE H. BLOEDEL, WILLIAMSTOWN, MASSACHUSETTS

GRACE BORGENICHT GALLERY, NEW YORK

BOWDOIN COLLEGE LIBRARY

BOWDOIN COLLEGE MUSEUM OF ART

MR. NATHAN CHAIKEN, NEW YORK

THE CHASE MANHATTAN BANK, NEW YORK

THE DETROIT INSTITUTE OF ARTS

MR. WILLIAM C. ESTY, NEW YORK

MR. AND MRS. LAWRENCE FLEISCHMAN, DETROIT, MICHIGAN

MR. MALCOLM GOLDSTEIN, NEW YORK

MR. CHARLES GWATHMEY, NEW YORK

MR. AND MRS. JULIUS S. HELD, NEW YORK

THE JOSEPH H. HIRSHHORN COLLECTION, NEW YORK

DEPARTMENT OF PRINTING AND GRAPHIC ARTS,

HARVARD COLLEGE LIBRARY

MR. AND MRS. PHILIP HOFER, CAMBRIDGE, MASSACHUSETTS

MR. HAROLD HUGO, MERIDEN, CONNECTICUT

MR. AND MRS. PHILIP M. ISAACSON, LEWISTON, MAINE

MRS. JACOB M. KAPLAN, NEW YORK

MR. AND MRS. SIDNEY KINGSLEY, NEW YORK

KRANNERT ART MUSEUM, UNIVERSITY OF ILLINOIS, URBANA

MRS. KATHARINE KUH, NEW YORK

MR. AND MRS. HERBERT C. LEE, BELMONT, MASSACHUSETTS

MR. JAY C. LEFF, UNIONTOWN, PENNSYLVANIA

DR. AND MRS. S. LIFSCHUTZ, NEW BRUNSWICK, NEW JERSEY

MR. AND MRS. HOWARD W. LIPMAN, NEW YORK

MR. AND MRS. ALBERT A. LIST, NEW YORK

DR. AND MRS. ABRAHAM MELAMED, MILWAUKEE, WISCONSIN

MRS. G. MAC CULLOCH MILLER, NEW YORK

BORIS MIRSKI GALLERY, BOSTON

MUNSON-WILLIAMS-PROCTOR INSTITUTE, UTICA, NEW YORK

NEW SCHOOL FOR SOCIAL RESEARCH, NEW YORK

MR. LEE NORDNESS, NEW YORK

MR. AND MRS. FRANCIS M. O'BRIEN, PORTLAND, MAINE

MR. AND MRS. LEON POMERANCE, GREAT NECK, NEW YORK

PRIVATE COLLECTION, NEW YORK

MR. SELDEN RODMAN (INSIDERS MUSEUM), OAKLAND, NEW JERSEY

MR. LESSING J. ROSENWALD, ALVERTHORPE GALLERY,

JENKINTOWN, PENNSYLVANIA

ST. JOHN'S ABBEY, COLLEGEVILLE, MINNESOTA

MR. AND MRS. JACOB SCHULMAN, GLOVERSVILLE, NEW YORK

MRS. MARGARETE SCHULTZ, GREAT NECK, NEW YORK

MR. AND MRS. HERMAN D. SHICKMAN, ROCKVILLE CENTRE, NEW YORK

MR. AND MRS. HERBERT M. SINGER, NEW YORK

SMITH COLLEGE MUSEUM OF ART, NORTHAMPTON, MASSACHUSETTS

MR. M. J. STEWART, WILTON, CONNECTICUT

STEPHEN AND SYBIL STONE FOUNDATION,

NEWTON CENTRE, MASSACHUSETTS

MR. AND MRS. ARTHUR VERSHBOW, NEWTON CENTRE, MASSACHUSETTS

WHITNEY MUSEUM OF AMERICAN ART (LIVING ARTS

FOUNDATION FUND), NEW YORK

ANONYMOUS LENDER

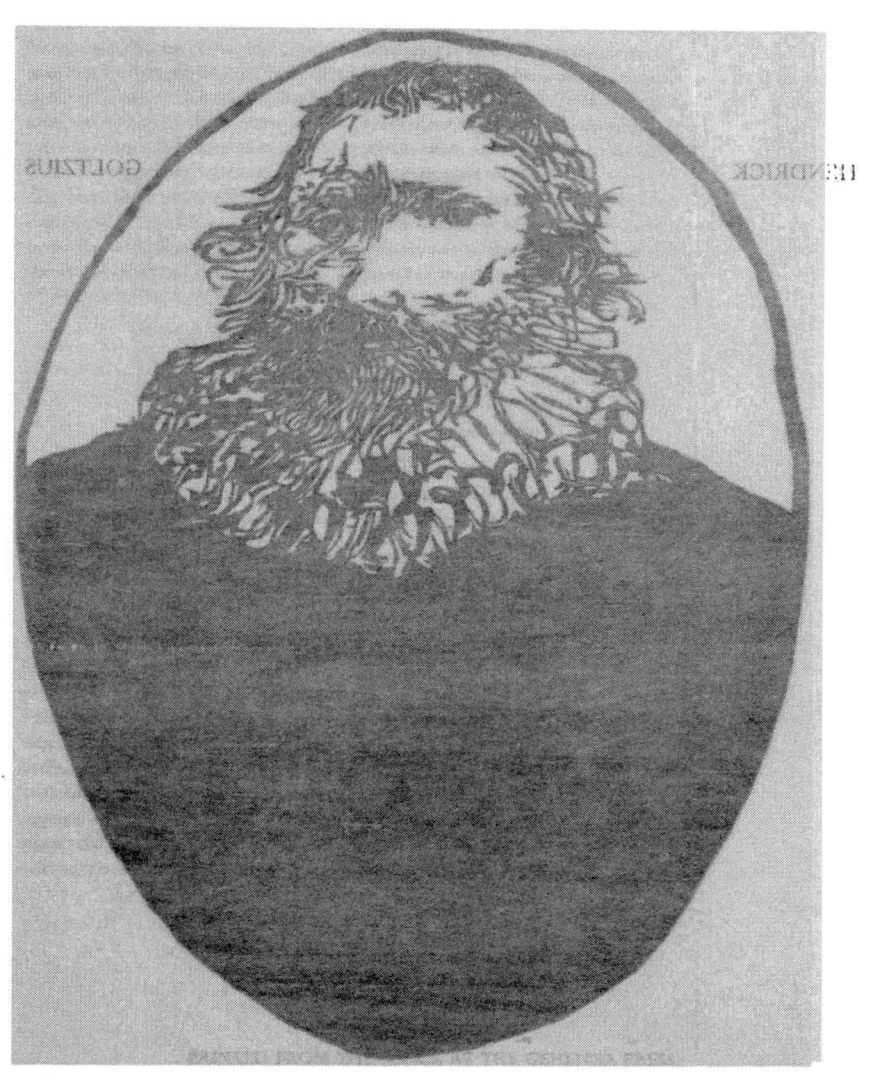

GOLTZIUS   HENDRICK

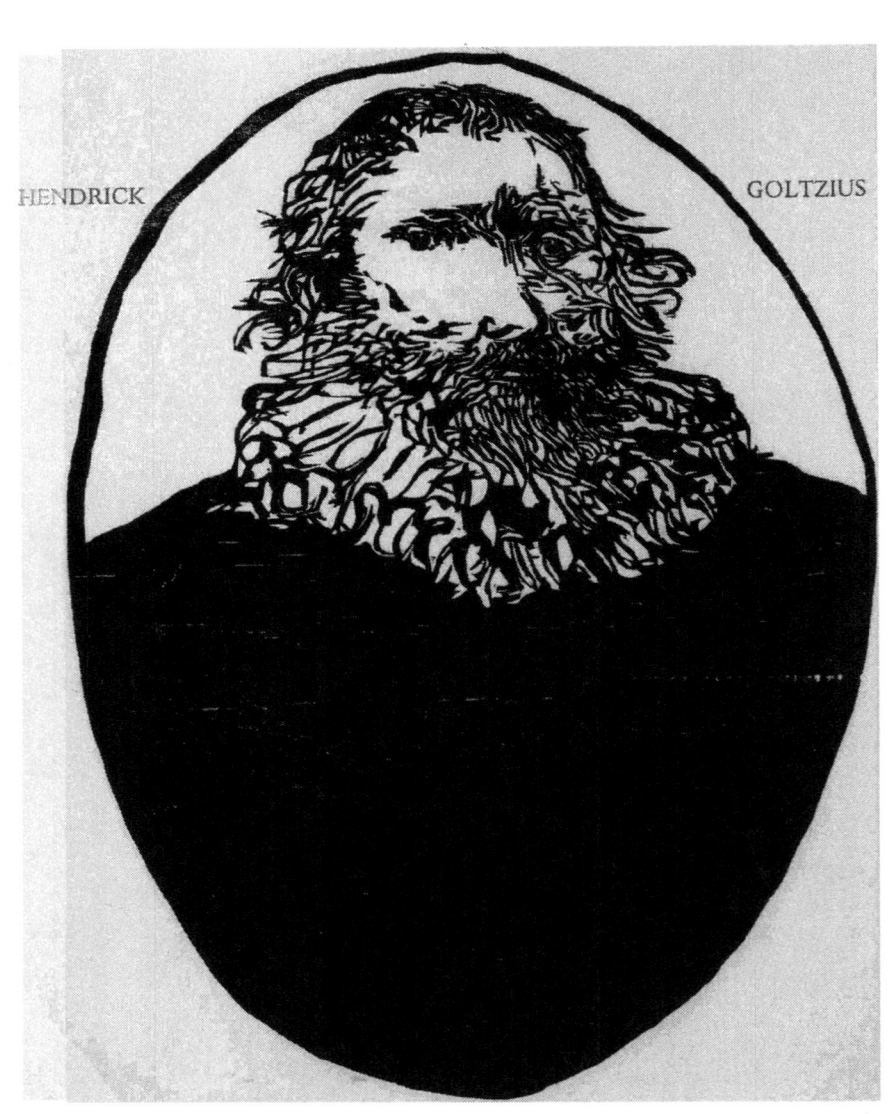

HENDRICK   GOLTZIUS

he did so not as a voyeur or as a feaster on the human edure, [...] levels poetry. When Shakespeare spoke of 'bones' being 'coral [...] diving not for corruption but for splendor. When Grünewald pa [...] Christ's brow red and green, he achieved the radiancy of a flower [...] The more of flesh and color and fire is that of life against death [...] against death, an iconography of age against eternal chaos. It even [...] tion if the readers of death could never be overwhelmed by [...] line which depicts art. Dare Poston, I see every that Max Abinolen [...] profession for a class of mothers that are wholly supply to by [...] today? For we are unworthy to calculate's power, because the [...] world, in terms of our takes. [...] embraces us as its own. [...] vanquished, the fierce, and which portions of the triumph, for [...] oppress his authentic perception of malignance and is thus not [...] mocks and defeats death while outliving its image. It is a fact that malignant life has turned him shockingly, and that to this he has answered with style. Does, forbid-

PRINTED FROM THE BLOCK AT THE GEHENNA PRESS

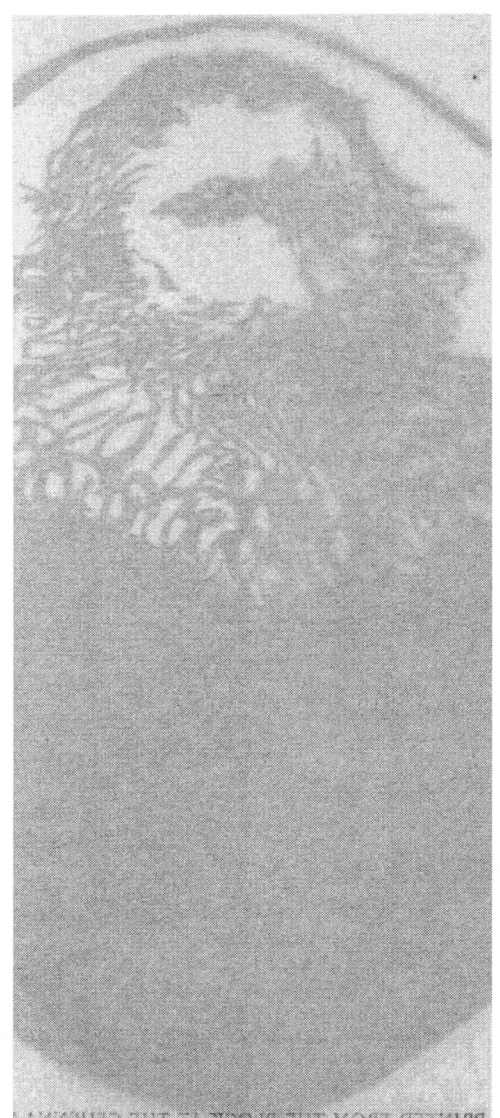

INTRODUCTION. Once when I told Baskin that if skill and experience were transferable commodities, I would want to bequeath mine to him to make him even more of a portent than he is, he rumbled quietly, that I already had. I do not believe we will ever give up the pleasure of indulging in such affectionate extravagances with each other; and if I repeat that episode it is only because I intend to declare the nature of a relationship which makes me unashamedly, and without compunction, a friend and partisan of his art. I shall not write therefore the impartial and historical thesis meant to prove his importance in the world of vision. I shall only repeat once more that I am on his side because I was born to be so, and that, therefore, nothing more can be expected from me on this occasion except the expression of unconditional and full-voiced endorsement of what he is. ✛ I will permit myself only a brief commentary on subject matter, simply because it may clarify a situation and reveal him fairly. He has often been berated for his adoption of death as a theme. When Donne wrote

> 'Then, as all my soules bee,
> Emparadis'd in you, (in whom alone
> I understand, and grow and see,)
> The rafters of my body, bone
> Being still with you, the Muscle, Sinew, and Veine,
> Which tile this house, will come againe.'

he did so not as a voyeur or as a fetishist of the human edifice, but as a maker of lovely poetry. When Shakespeare spoke of 'bones' being 'coral made', he was skin diving not for corruption but for splendor. When Grunewald painted the body of Christ sinister red and green, he achieved the radiance of a flower bed at twilight. The story of form and color and line is that of life against death; life, or existence, against death, or nothingness; design against personal chaos. It only remains to be seen if the subject of death itself cannot be overwhelmed by the very life of the line which depicts it. Does Baskin's line carry that life? A hundred times yes. ✛ A preference for a stated subject, the use of an assertive style, what anathema for today! For we are supposed to add with desperate elegance to the quandary of our world, in terms of a quandary of non-resolution and non-style. Then the world embraces us as its own darlings whose utterances have the authenticity of the victimized, the frothy and ample gestures of the drowned. ✛ Against this, Baskin opposes his authentic pretention and resolution not to be a victim; in truth his line mocks and defeats death while outlining its image. It is a fact that malicious fate has taunted him shockingly, and that to this he has answered with style. Dour, forbidding, and entire, this style, while depicting terror, is not the prey of terror. Others, who paint the bright and vague maps of fashion to hide in them, are, in fact, the dupes of the terror of seeing themselves identified. Are we so simple that we don't sniff the odor of general and impersonal death of the spirit also in the yards of vermilion and ultramarine of our latest Biennial? ✒ Take Baskin's prophecy out of the contemporary scene and the world of art would be suddenly less oppres- sive, sillier, and destitute.

RICO LEBRUN

SCULPTURE. At forty, Leonard Baskin can look back on a career that began slowly and with many a strange detour, only to take wings suddenly and to soar to international prominence. In a letter which I received from him in 1953, the year that was most clearly marked by signs of widespread recognition, he said: 'Although it has been my prints which have won for me all this praise, my [real] and profound concern is for sculpture.' He was then working on the large *Man with Dead Bird* (Museum of Modern Art) which he began in 1951 in Babylon, Long Island, and finished in 1954 in his studio on Titan's Pier, South Hadley, Massachusetts. Despite some unresolved passages, especially in the movement of arms and hands, this piece marks Baskin's entrance into the ranks of major modern sculptors. ✷ He had done a good deal of sculpture before, ever since his early studies with Maurice Glickman at the Educational Alliance. Yet he had run into difficulties of various kinds. Attracted by wood from the beginning, he occasionally found his efforts thwarted by faulty conditions of his raw material. More important was that his early admiration for Rodin and Epstein caused him to think in terms of complex formal relationships and subtle surface effects which were unsuited for the projection of strong, simple messages. With the *Man with Dead Bird*, Baskin had found the laconic language of forms that he needed to convey his thoughts. ✷ It does not diminish the merits of this style if we recognize that it, too, is indebted to earlier artistic trends. While many of Baskin's contemporaries were frantically busy demonstrating their artistic independence, Baskin studied diligently, and indeed collected, the artistic records of the past. Like the great masters of the Renaissance and Baroque, he absorbed a variety of impressions and today commands a knowledge of the art of the past rarely matched even by art historians. There are some favorites, beginning with the Egyptians whom he first encountered as a boy in the Brooklyn Museum; he saw them again, as well as the Sumerians, in Paris and London during his year abroad in 1950–51. A visit to Pisa during that year was made memorable by the discovery of Giovanni Pisano and Tino da Camaino. Besides the study of originals, he derived enduring stimuli from books. His admiration for Barlach stems from a first encounter with the German sculptor in books seen at the New York Public Library. The unquiet tranquillity of death-masks was first experienced by Baskin in the pages of Benkard's *Das Ewige Antlitz*—and has haunted his art ever since. ✷ All these encounters served to release in him the demonic forces of his own creative energy. Sustained and enriched by a vast historical awareness and erudition, Baskin's art is thoroughly contemporary and entirely his own. It is an art committed to the propagation of a few basic themes, for which he has fought with words as well as works. These 'themes' are comprehensible only in terms of twentieth-century situations, political and social as much as artistic. Baskin's immediate concern is with 'meaning', with the projection of definite attitudes, be they friendly or hostile. Some of Baskin's sculptures appear as condensations of sinister forces, cast in the shape of bloated laureates, helmeted but faceless blackguards, gluttonous Epicureans and sensualists. Their favorite gestures are the folded arms of smug self-satisfaction, supporting the derisive bulk of enormous shoulders. Their ranks are swelled by a bestiary of malevolent creatures, crows, owls, and—mirroring a Talmudic antipathy—dogs. These figures are the objects of Baskin's scorn, the symbols of brutality, of tyranny, of pompous self-righteousness. They are the reincarnation of Goya's Monster of War, bestriding the world with ruthless power. ॐ At the opposite end of the scale are the figures of the dead, latter-day brothers of the 'gisants' of late medieval tombs, and perhaps indebted, in their earliest examples (ca. 1950) to Lehmbruck and Pompeian petrifactions. These figures give pathos and dignity to the theme of the 'victim'—not necessarily the victim of specific aggression, but of mortality in general. Most of them are naked, but the idea of the shroud, the benevolent wrapping for man's decaying corpse, has occupied Baskin from the early *John Donne* (inspired by a seventeenth-century sculpture) to the *Lazarus* of 1960 and the large *Dead Man* of 1961. The recurrent occupation with this theme demonstrates the suffusion, in Baskin's sculpture, of structural problems and preferences with intelligible meaning: the Miracle of Lazarus' revival is given visible immediacy through the manner in which the calm, smooth head emerges from the turbulence of the drapery like the polished core of a chestnut from the rough hulk of its peel. ॐ The contrasts of agitated and quiet surfaces are found in many variations and with different associations. In the head of *Bresdin* (1953–54) the aggressively faceted beard garlands and subtly stresses the quiet dignity of the face; in the *Homage to the Un-American Activities Committee* (1959) the soft, pathetic head of a 'victim' is contrasted frighteningly to formal uproar of a blustering bird-monster; and in the relief of *Isaac* (1959) the excited flutter of the wings makes more poignant the gentle, lyrical modulation of the boy's body. ॐ The *Isaac* relief belongs to a group of works for which Baskin himself pointed out his sources: 'The medals, Janson's *Donatello*, and G. Manzù have led me to a number of Bas-Reliefs very low and very Quattrocentesque' (letter of August 7, 1958). But it is also an example of Baskin's persistent efforts to achieve a pictorial condensation of specific meanings. *Isaac* is at once three different things: the beloved son, the horned victim, and the winged instrument of deliverance. Such composite images reflect not only the knowledge of masters of 'hybridization' like Bosch and Grünewald, but also of the tradition of emblematic illustration which has fascinated Baskin for many years. ॐ Baskin's sculpture clearly exemplifies the artist's general disdain for abstraction and any kind of formalism. Yet it stands also in opposition to the specific popular notion that the primary function of sculpture is realized in the interplay between solid shapes and open spaces. The best modern sculptors, undoubtedly, have derived exquisite formal patterns from this principle which they share with (and have possibly derived from) modern architecture. ✌ Baskin shuns this fashionable mode of expression. To him sculpture is above all the creation of cohesive bodies. His principal concern is with structural solidity, wholeness, and strength. His respect for bodily integrity prompts him to simplify and to reduce in importance details such as mouths, noses, and ears and to indicate eyes by lightly incised lines. His marked preference for bald types springs from the same stylistic root. The surface patterns caused by the varying grains of his laminated woods—though occasionally quite attractive—are coincidental rather than planned, and they are never essential. ✌ If the *Man with Dead Bird* was the first clear manifestation of this style, the huge *Grieving Angel* represents one of its most harmonious formulations. Despite its size and majestic bearing the figure is informed with a spirit of tenderness, a kind of austere compassion, that reveals an aspect of Baskin's nature rarely permitted to show but all the more welcome when it does. Nor does it constrain the beholder to a limited number of positions from which to look at the piece, a restriction which is particularly noticeable in enthroned figures of severe frontality such as the *Man with Owl* (1959, Smith College) and the *Seated Woman*. ✌ In his latest major work of sculpture, *St. Thomas Aquinas*, Baskin appears to strike out in new directions. Still stressing the inviolable quality of the block, the artist allows his figure a greater degree of freedom of motion, here impressively suggestive of an incisive if somewhat arrogant intellectual activity. The analogy with hieratic cult-images no longer appears to hold true. The torsion of the body is accentuated by undulating masses of drapery which resemble waves breaking around a promontory as they roll towards the proudly raised head. After ten years of perfecting a style of monumental, if archaic grandeur, Baskin now seems to stand where Greek sculpture stood at the beginning of its 'classical' period. His past achievements hold still greater promise for the future.

JULIUS S. HELD,
Barnard
College

SCULPTURE

1.
RODOLPHE BRESDIN
Machaerium, 1954, h. 12 ¼ ins.
Mr. and Mrs. Leon Pomerance
Great Neck, New York

2.
WILLIAM BLAKE
Bronze, 1955, h. 7 ¼
Mr. and Mrs. Herbert M. Singer
New York

3.
JOHN DONNE IN HIS WIND-
ING CLOTH
Bronze, 1955, h. 21
Mr. and Mrs. Arthur Vershbow
Newton Centre, Massachusetts

4.
SEATED FAT MAN
Bronze, 1956, h. 12 ½
Mr. and Mrs. Julius S. Held
New York

5.
HANGED MAN
Bronze, 1956, h. 7 ½
Mr. and Mrs. Howard W. Lipman
New York

6.
ESTHER
Bronze, 1956, h. 8 ¾
Mrs. Leonard Baskin
Northampton, Massachusetts

7.
LAUREATE STANDING
Cherry, 1957, h. 36
Dr. and Mrs. Abraham Melamed
Milwaukee, Wisconsin

8.
GRIEVING ANGEL
Walnut, 1958, h. 76 ¼
Munson-Williams-Proctor Institute
Utica, New York

9.
CROW
Bronze relief, 1958, 12 × 17 ½
The Detroit Institute of Arts
Detroit, Michigan

10.
DOG AND THISTLE
Bronze relief, 1958, 8 ½ × 8 ¼
Grace Borgenicht Gallery
New York

11.
"QUI M'AIME, AIME MON
CHIEN"
Bronze relief, 1958, 6 ½ × 8
Mrs. Margarete Schultz
Great Neck, New York

12.
MAN WITH OWL
Cherry, 1959, h. 30
Smith College Museum of Art
Northampton, Massachusetts

13.
OWL
Pine, 1959, h. 20 ½
Mrs. Jacob M. Kaplan
New York

14.
ISAAC
Bronze relief, 1959, 23 × 19
Krannert Art Museum
University of Illinois, Urbana

15.
BARLACH: DEAD
Poplar, 1959, h. 18
Dr. and Mrs. S. Lifschutz
New Brunswick, New Jersey

16.
HOMAGE TO GUSTAV
MAHLER
Bronze relief, 1959, 21 × 11
Grace Borgenicht Gallery
New York

17.
IN MEMORY OF LOUIS
BLACK
Bronze relief, 1959, 8 ½ × 17 ½
Mr. and Mrs. Julius S. Held
New York

18.
HOMAGE TO THE UN-
AMERICAN ACTIVITIES
COMMITTEE
Bronze relief, 1959, 12 × 11 ¼
Smith College Museum of Art
Northampton, Massachusetts

19.
THISTLE
Bronze relief, 1959, 22 × 16
Rabbi and Mrs. Samuel Baskin
New York

20.
GLUTTED DEATH
Bronze relief, 1959, 16 ½ × 8
Grace Borgenicht Gallery
New York

21.
LAZARUS
Bronze, 1960, h. 31 ¼
Mr. Selden Rodman
Insiders Museum, Oakland, New Jersey

22.
THOMAS EAKINS
Maple, 1960, h. 27
Mr. and Mrs. Lawrence Fleischman
Detroit, Michigan

23.
MAN WITH OWL
Walnut, 1960, h. 19
Mr. and Mrs. Herman D. Shickman
Rockville Centre, New York

24.
OWL
Bronze, 1960, h. 20
The Chase Manhattan Bank
New York

25.
STANDING CROW
Pine, 1960, h. 47
Mr. and Mrs. Herbert C. Lee
Belmont, Massachusetts

26.
BIRDMAN
Bronze, 1961, h. 35
Grace Borgenicht Gallery
New York

27.
DEATH
Bronze, 1961, h. 20
Mr. and Mrs. Albert A. List
New York

28.
DEAD MAN
Plaster, 1961 (*Bronze*, 1962), l. 72
Grace Borgenicht Gallery
New York

29.
SEATED WOMAN
Oak, 1961, h. 54
Grace Borgenicht Gallery
New York

30.
EAKINS
Copper relief, 1961, 12 ¼ × 8 ½
Grace Borgenicht Gallery
New York

31.
DENTATE ART NOUVEAU
FLOWER
Bronze relief, 1961, diameter 9
Grace Borgenicht Gallery
New York

32.
DEAD CROW
Bronze relief, 1961, 19 ½ × 40
Mr. Lawrence H. Bloedel
Williamstown, Massachusetts

33.
ARMOURED MAN
Birch, 1962, h. 29 ½
New School for Social Research
New York

34.
BENEVOLENT ANGEL
Birch, 1962, h. 29
Mr. and Mrs. Jacob Schulman
Gloversville, New York

35.
ST. THOMAS AQUINAS
Walnut, 1962, h. 39
St. John's Abbey
Collegeville, Minnesota

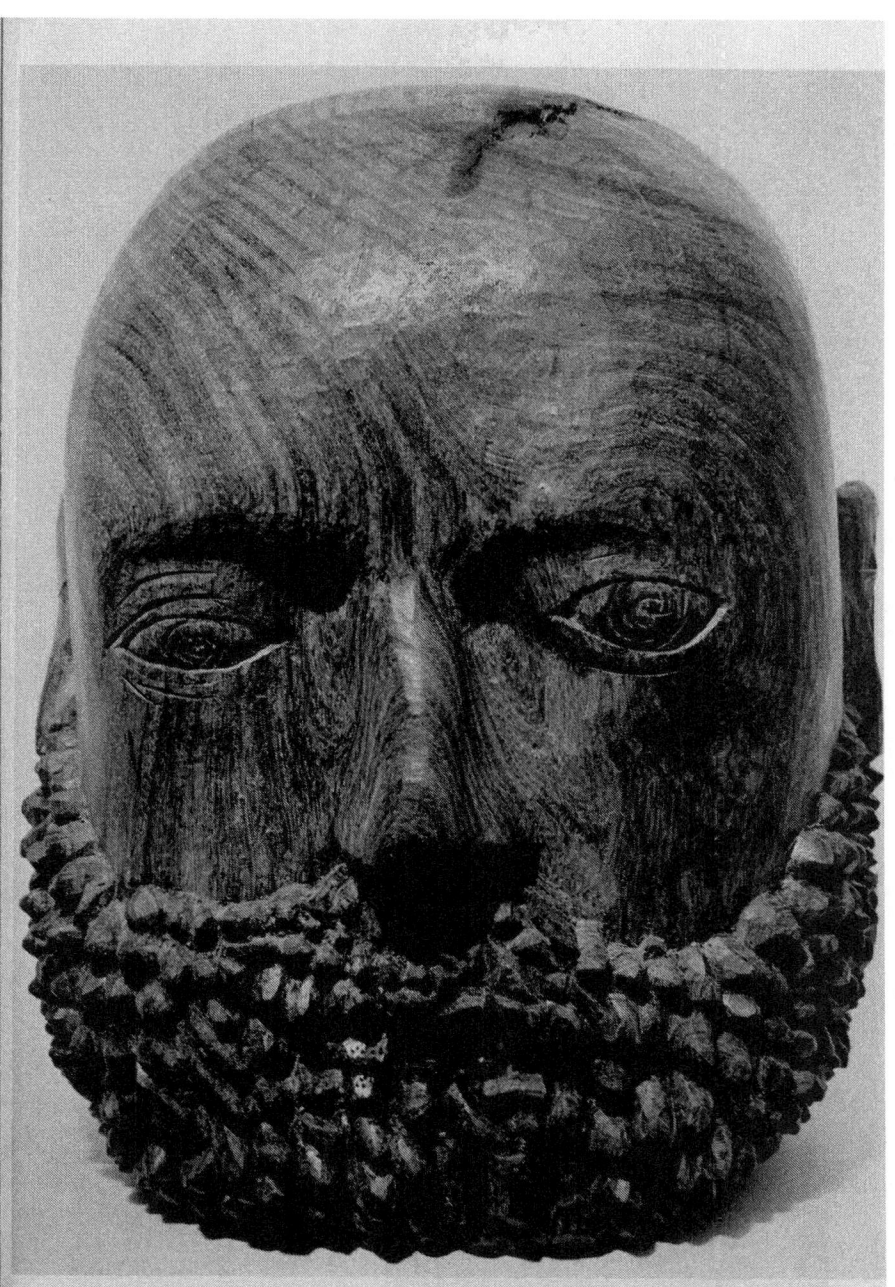

I. RODOLPHE BRESDIN, MACHAERIUM, 1954

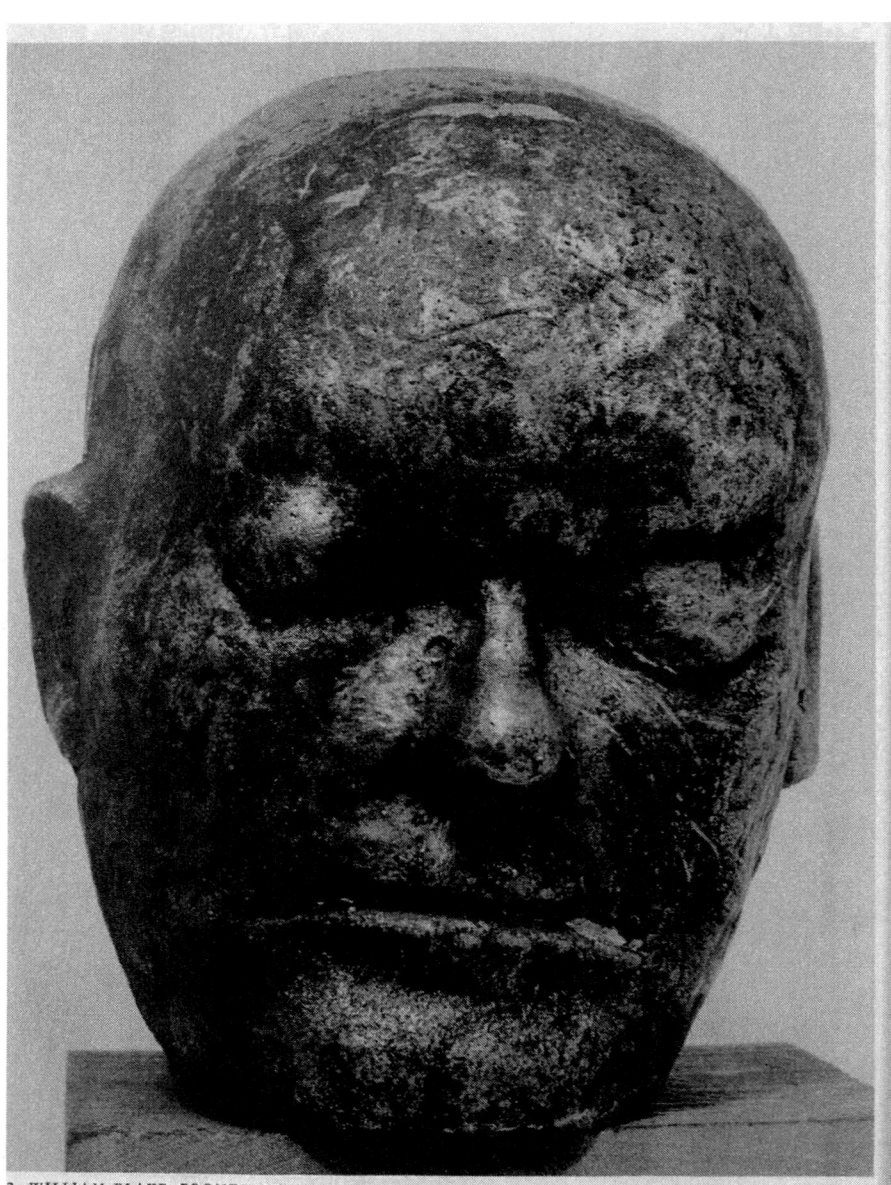

2. WILLIAM BLAKE, BRONZE, 1955

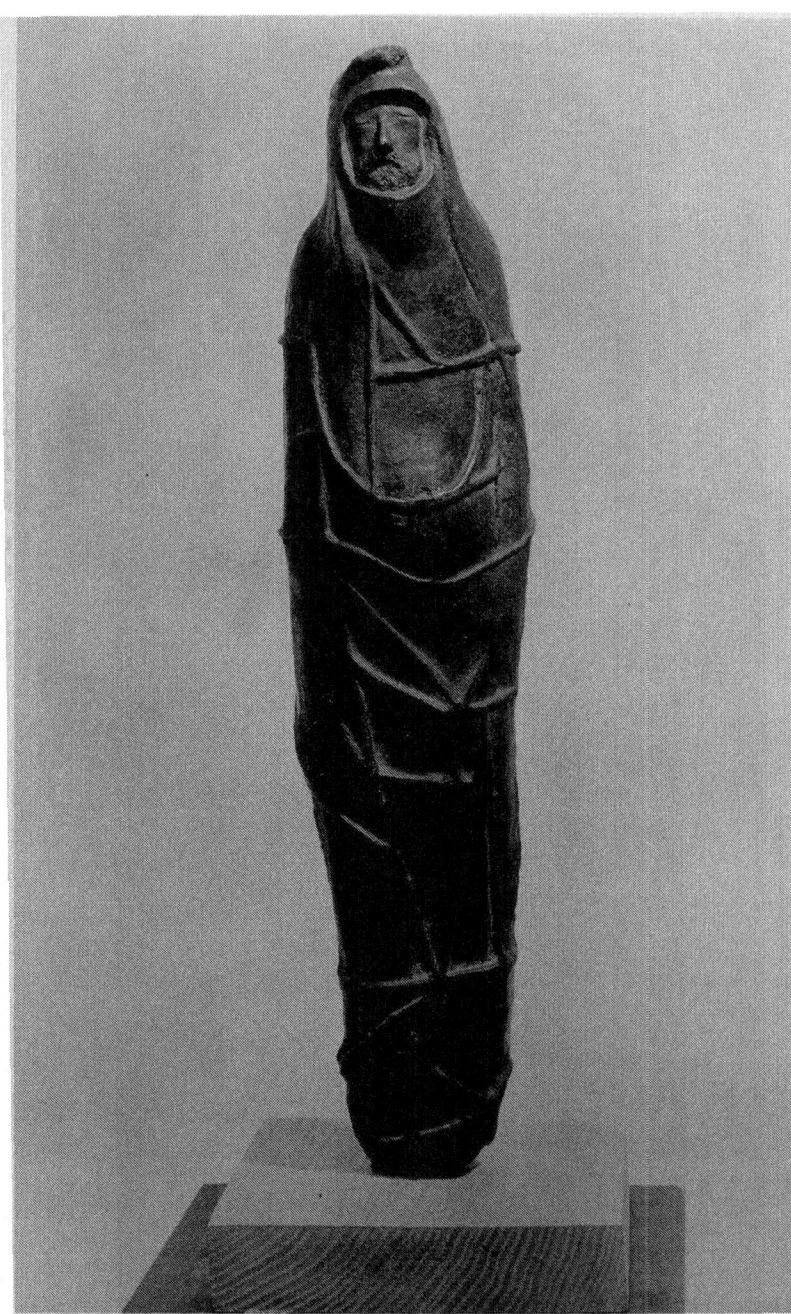

3. JOHN DONNE IN HIS WINDING CLOTH, BRONZE, 1955

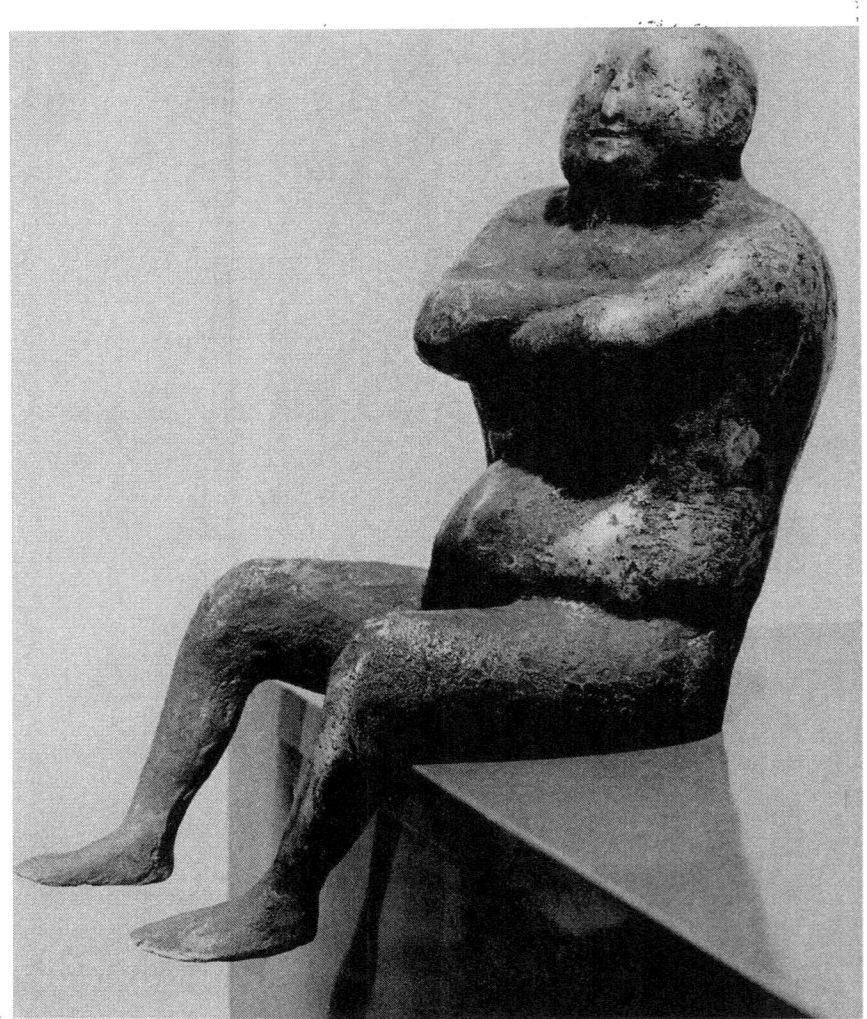

4. SEATED FAT MAN, BRONZE, 1956

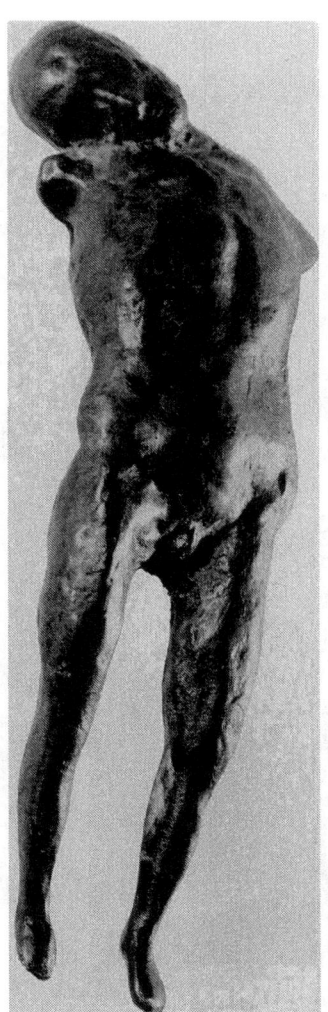

5. HANGED MAN, BRONZE, 1956

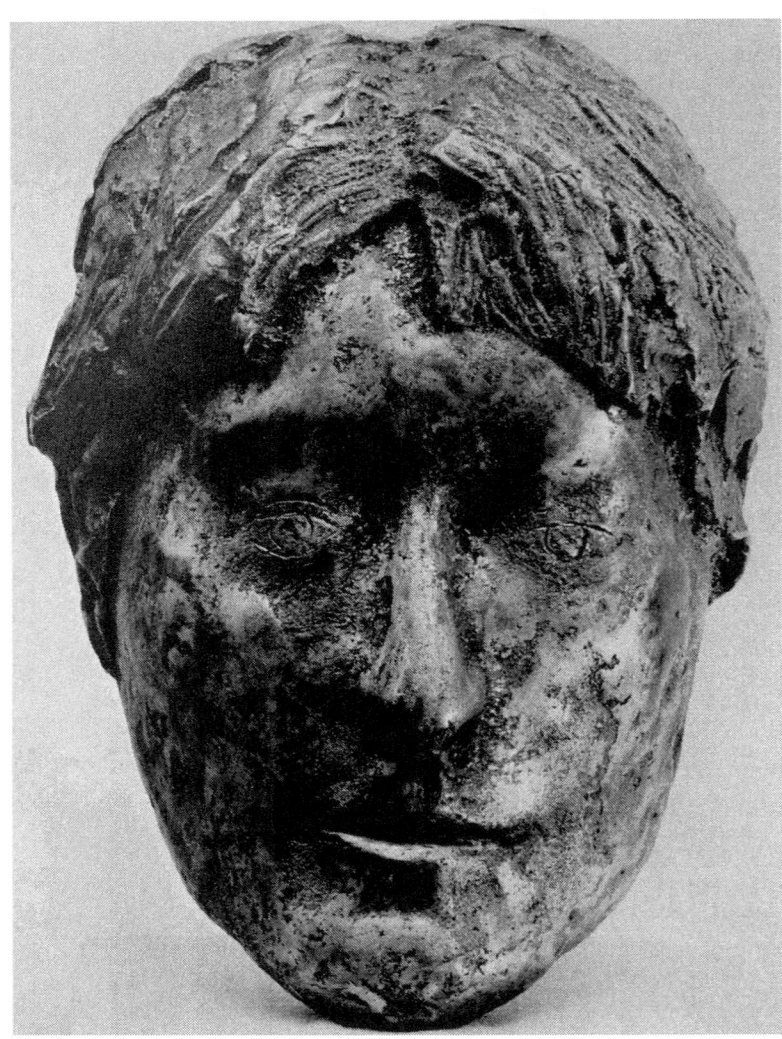

6. ESTHER, BRONZE, 1956

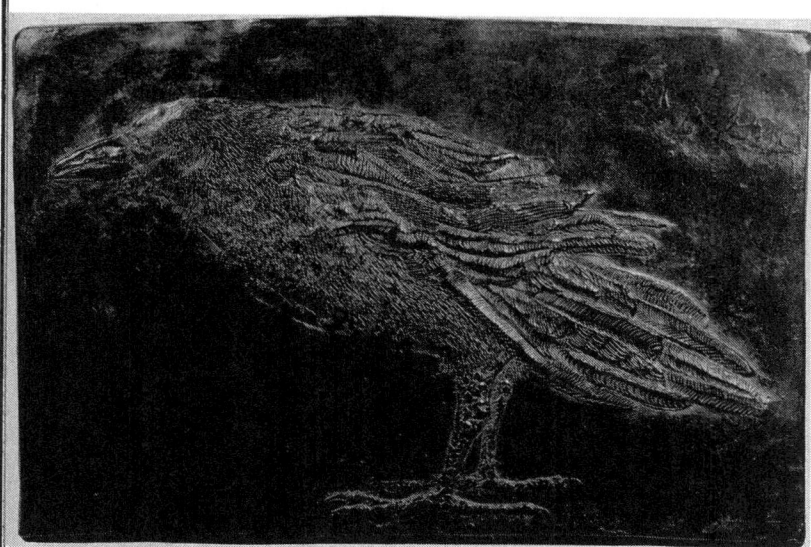

9. CROW, BRONZE RELIEF, 1958

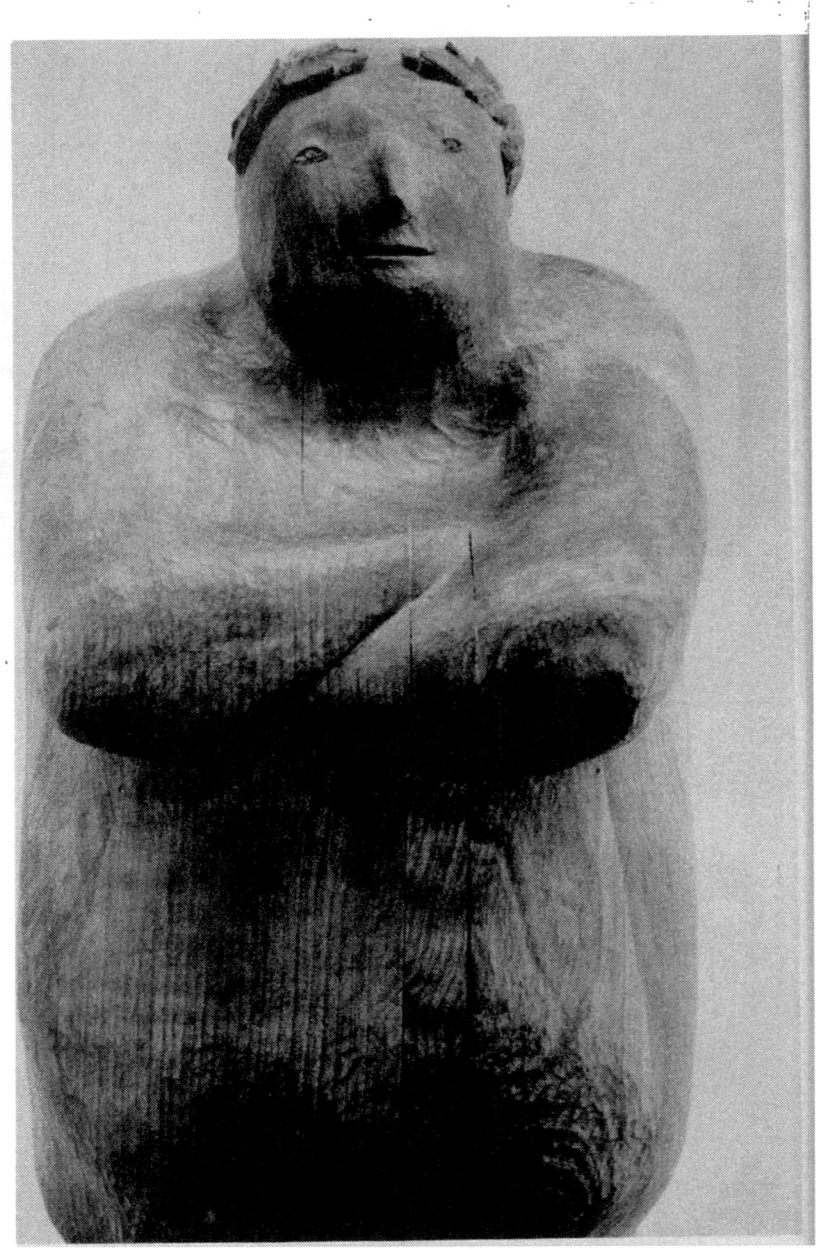

7. LAUREATE STANDING, CHERRY, 1957

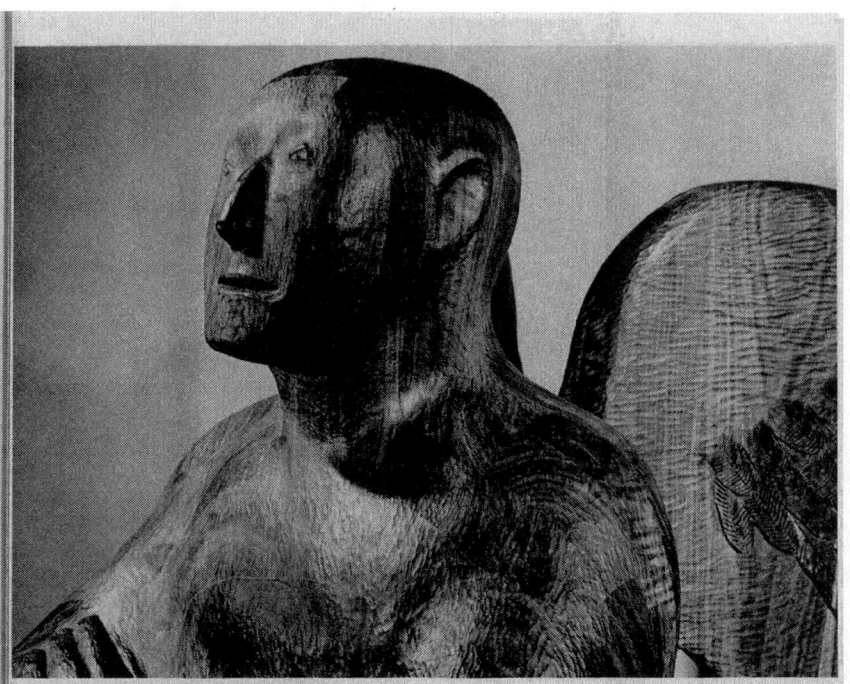

8. GRIEVING ANGEL, WALNUT, 1958

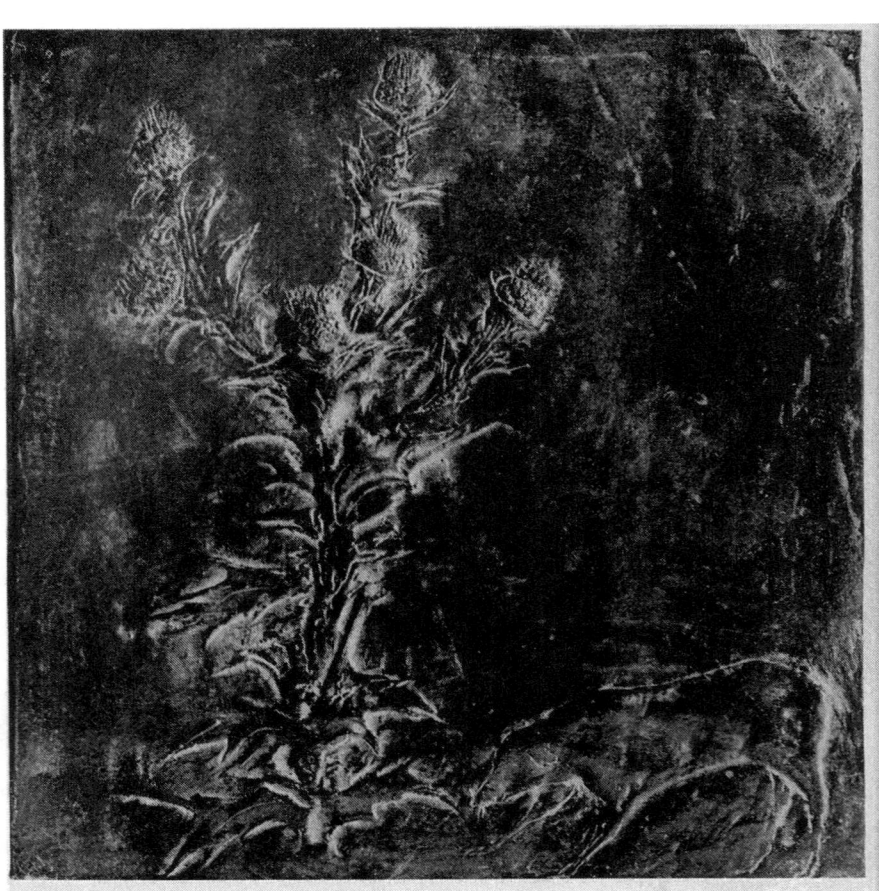

10. DOG AND THISTLE, BRONZE RELIEF, 1958

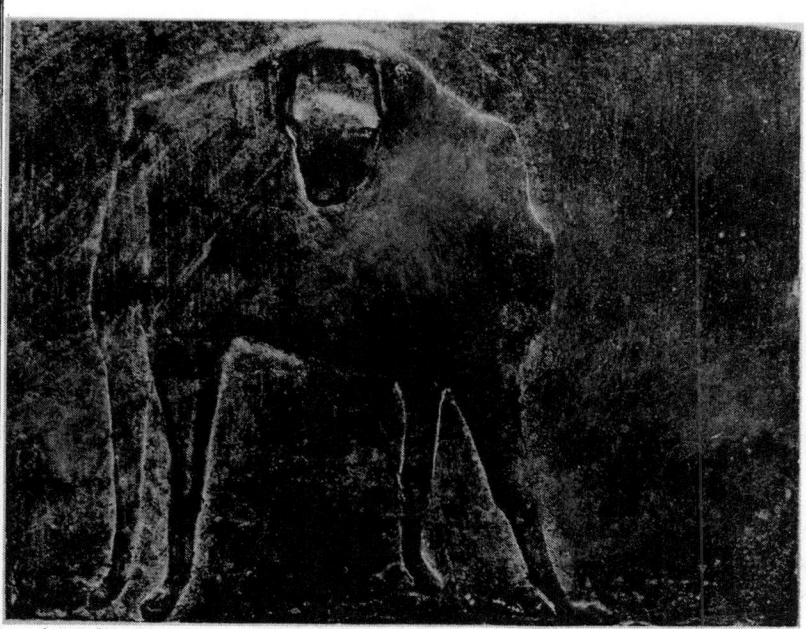

11. 'QUI M'AIME, AIME MON CHIEN', BRONZE RELIEF, 1958

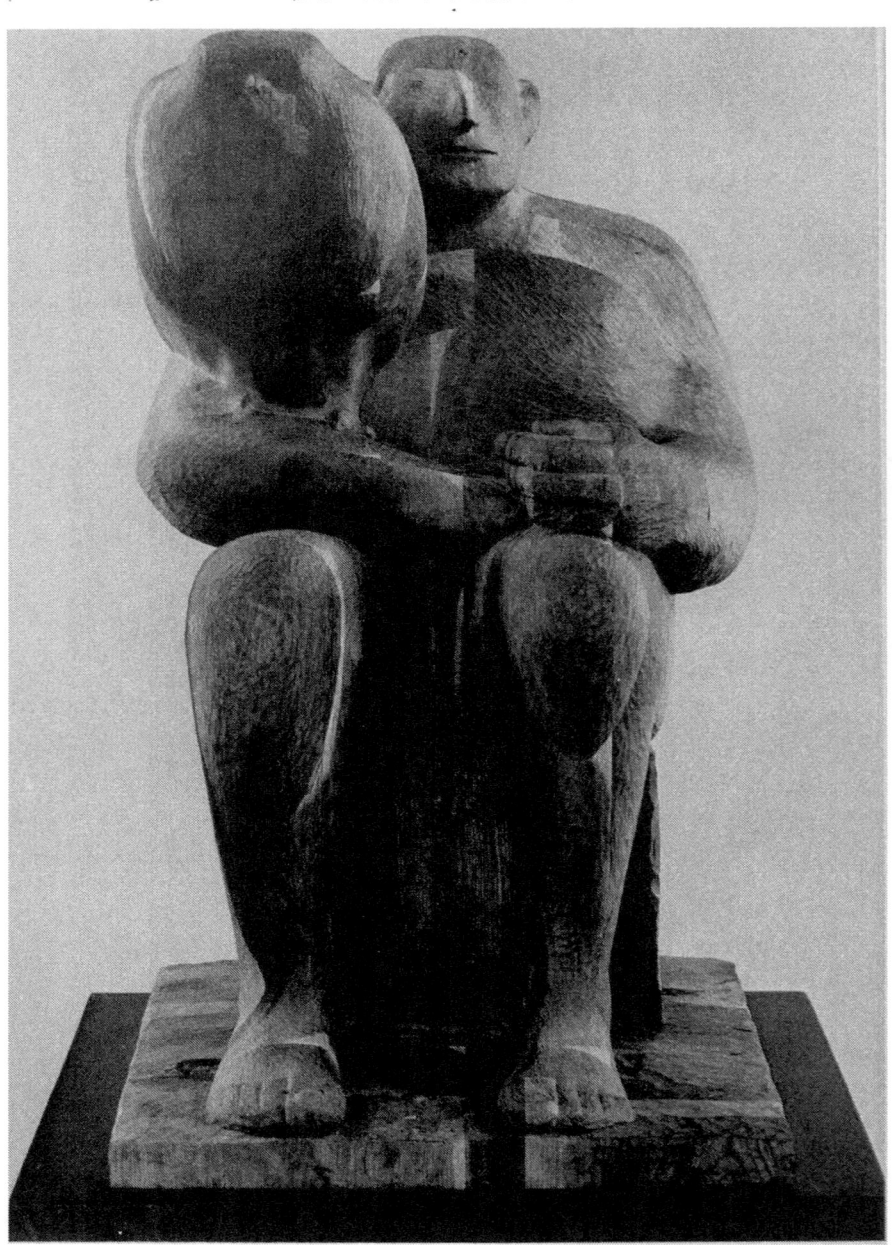

12. MAN WITH OWL, CHERRY, 1959

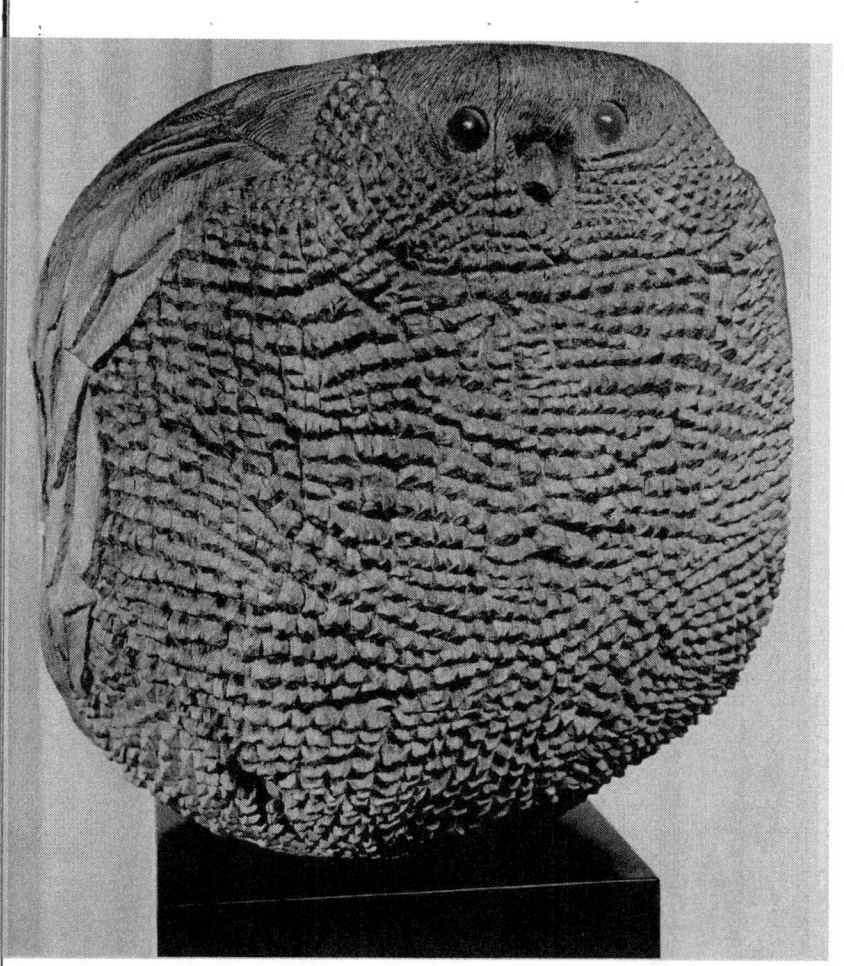

13. OWL, PINE, 1959

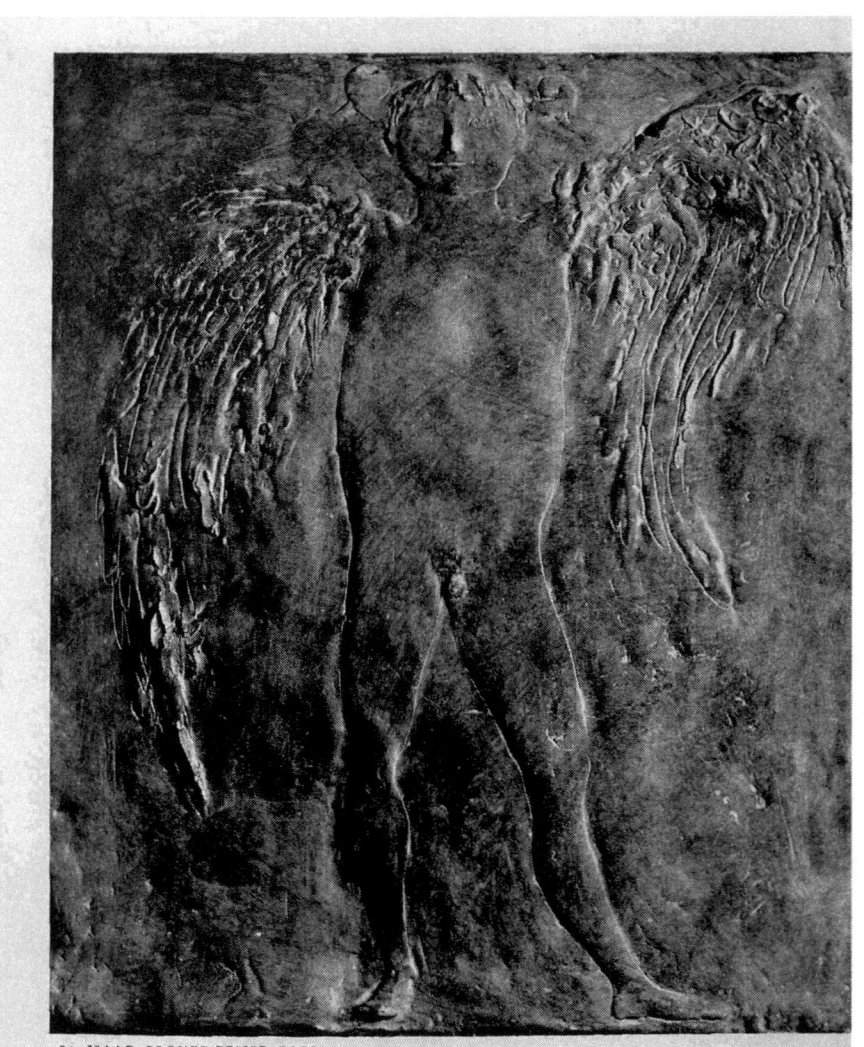

14. ISAAC, BRONZE RELIEF, 1959

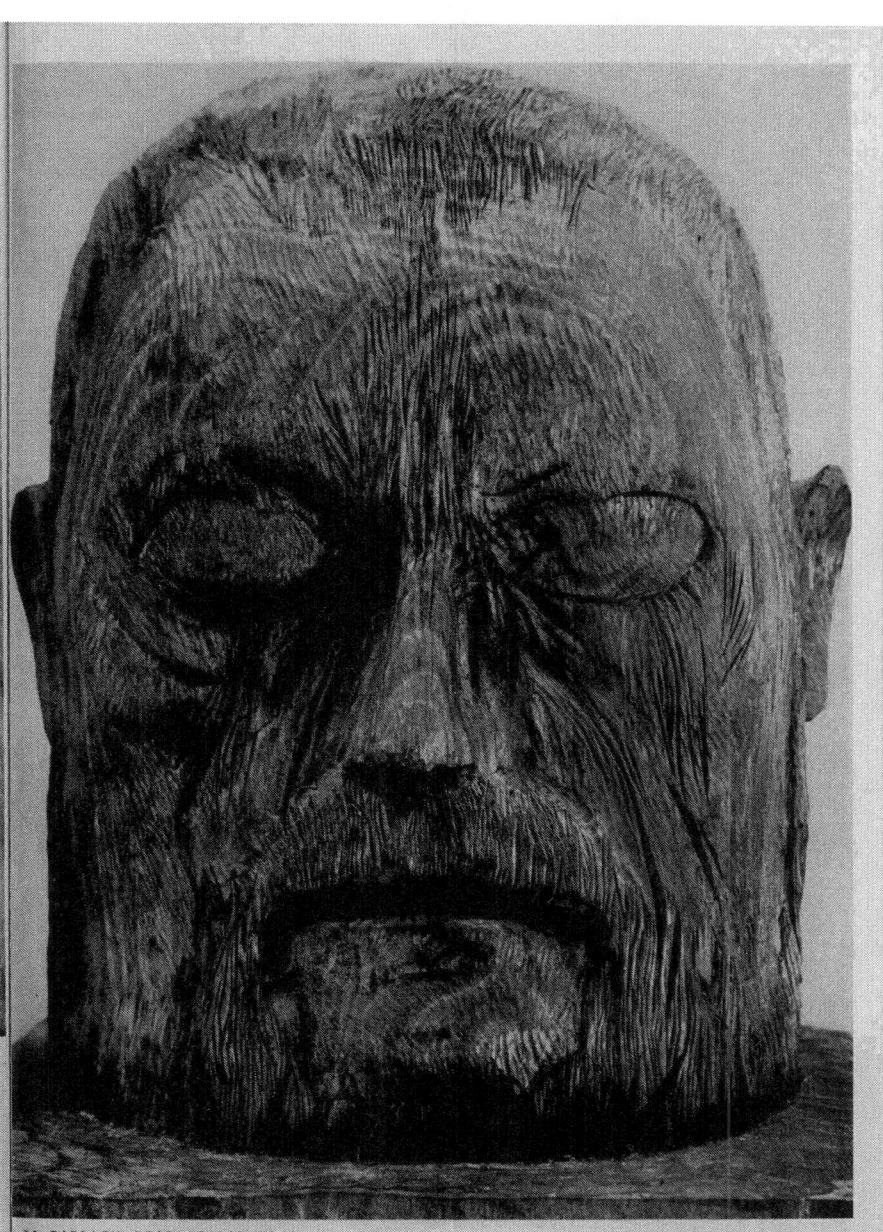

15. BARLACH: DEAD, POPLAR, 1959

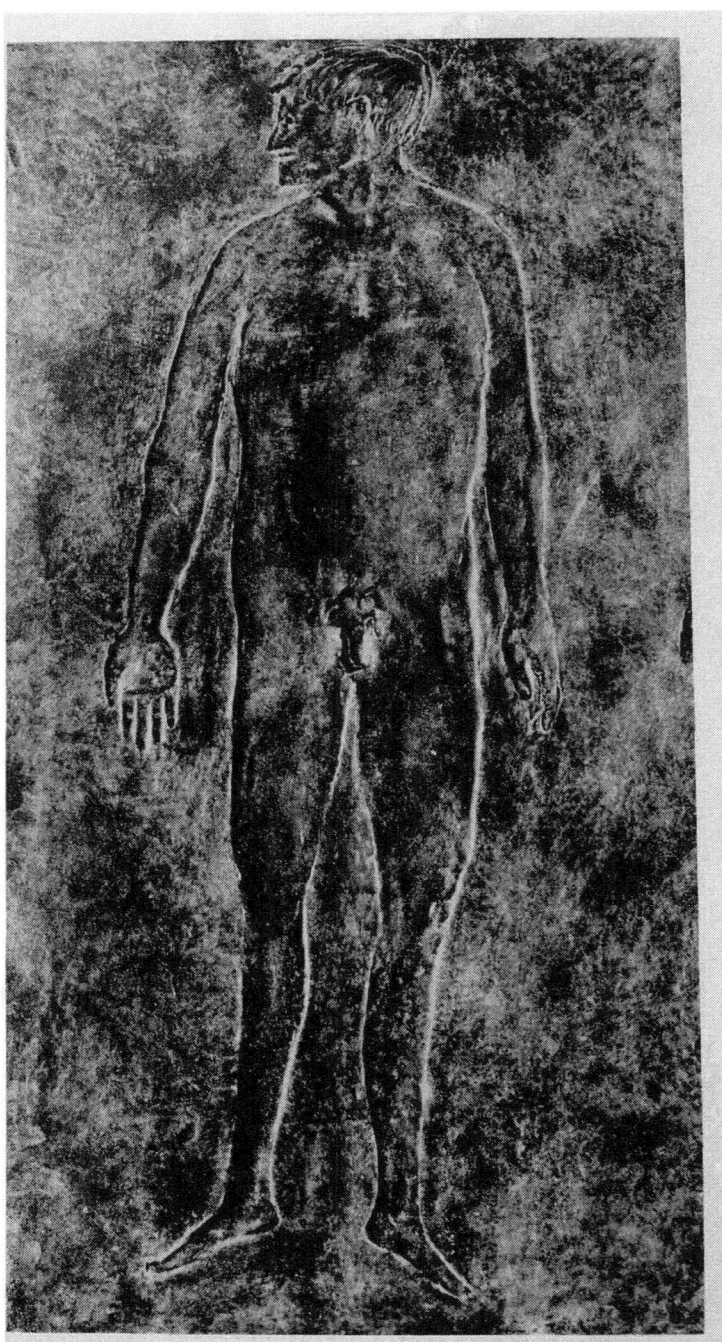

16. HOMAGE TO GUSTAV MAHLER, BRONZE RELIEF, 1959

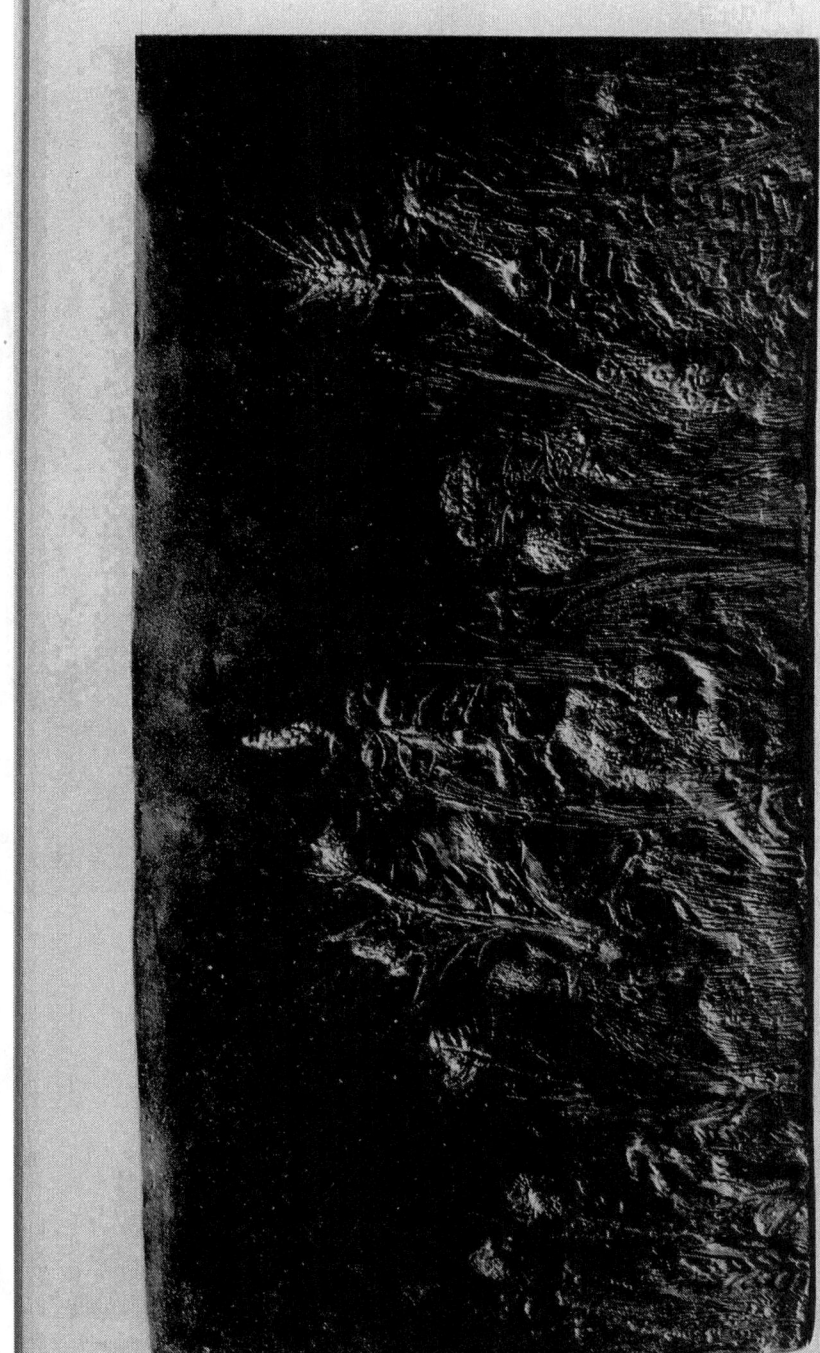

17. IN MEMORY OF LOUIS BLACK, BRONZE RELIEF, 1959

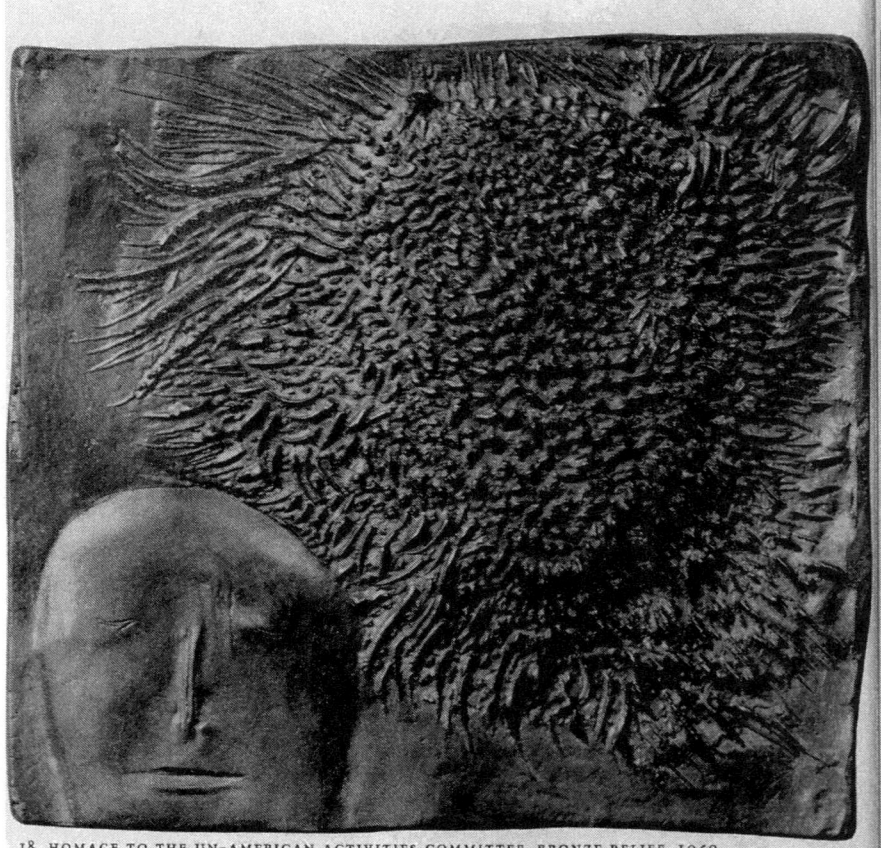

18. HOMAGE TO THE UN-AMERICAN ACTIVITIES COMMITTEE, BRONZE RELIEF, 1959

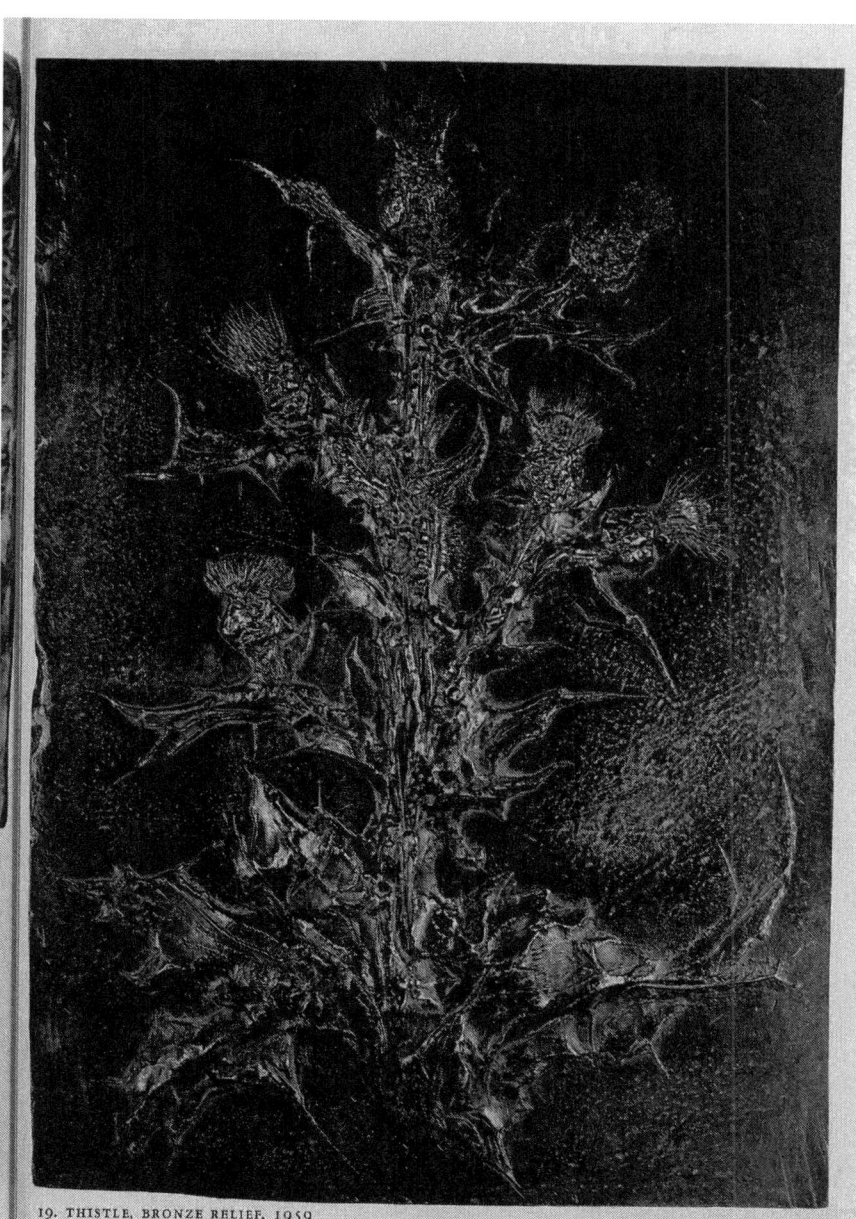

19. THISTLE, BRONZE RELIEF, 1959

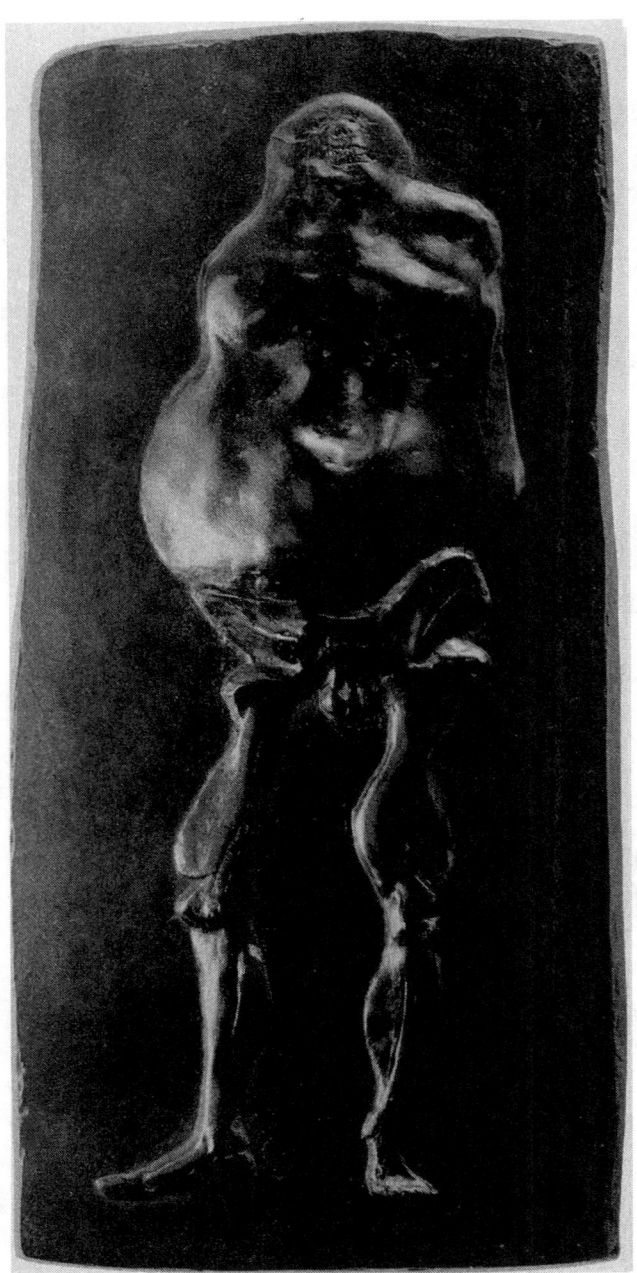

20. GLUTTED DEATH, BRONZE RELIEF, 1959

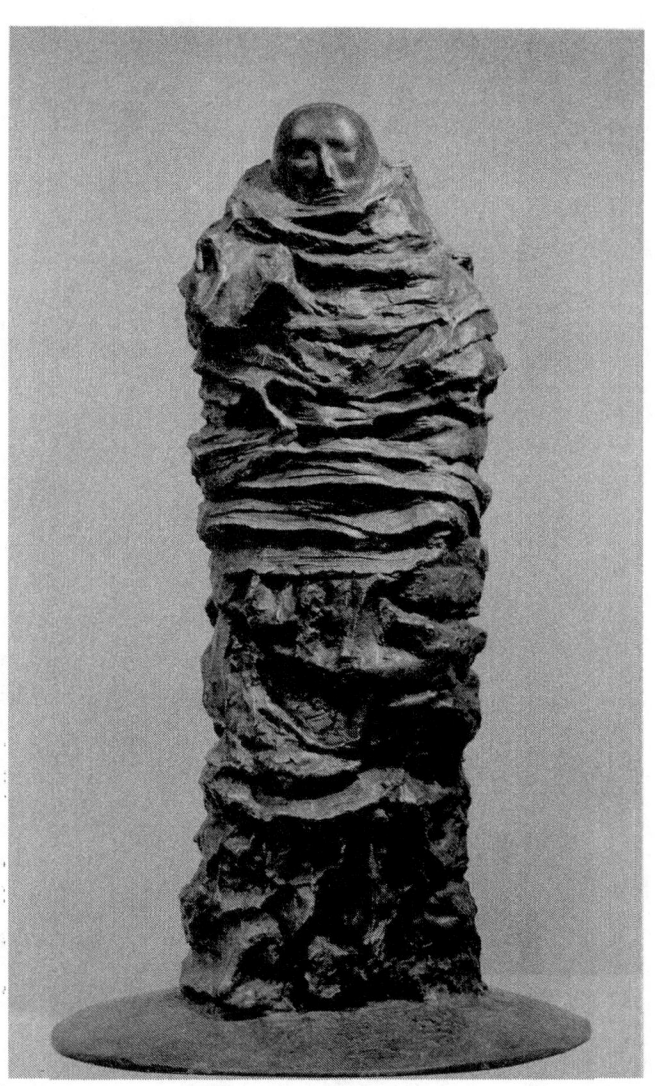

21. LAZARUS, BRONZE, 1960

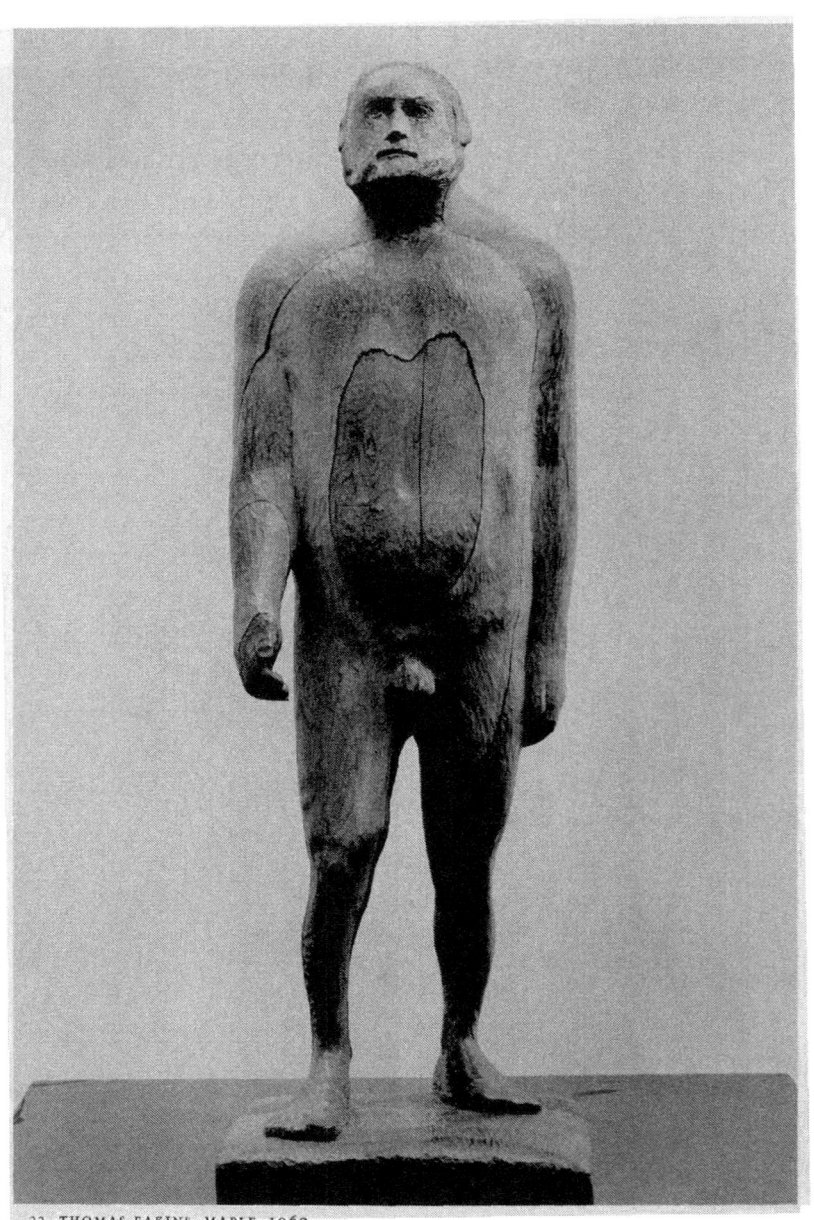

22. THOMAS EAKINS, MAPLE, 1960

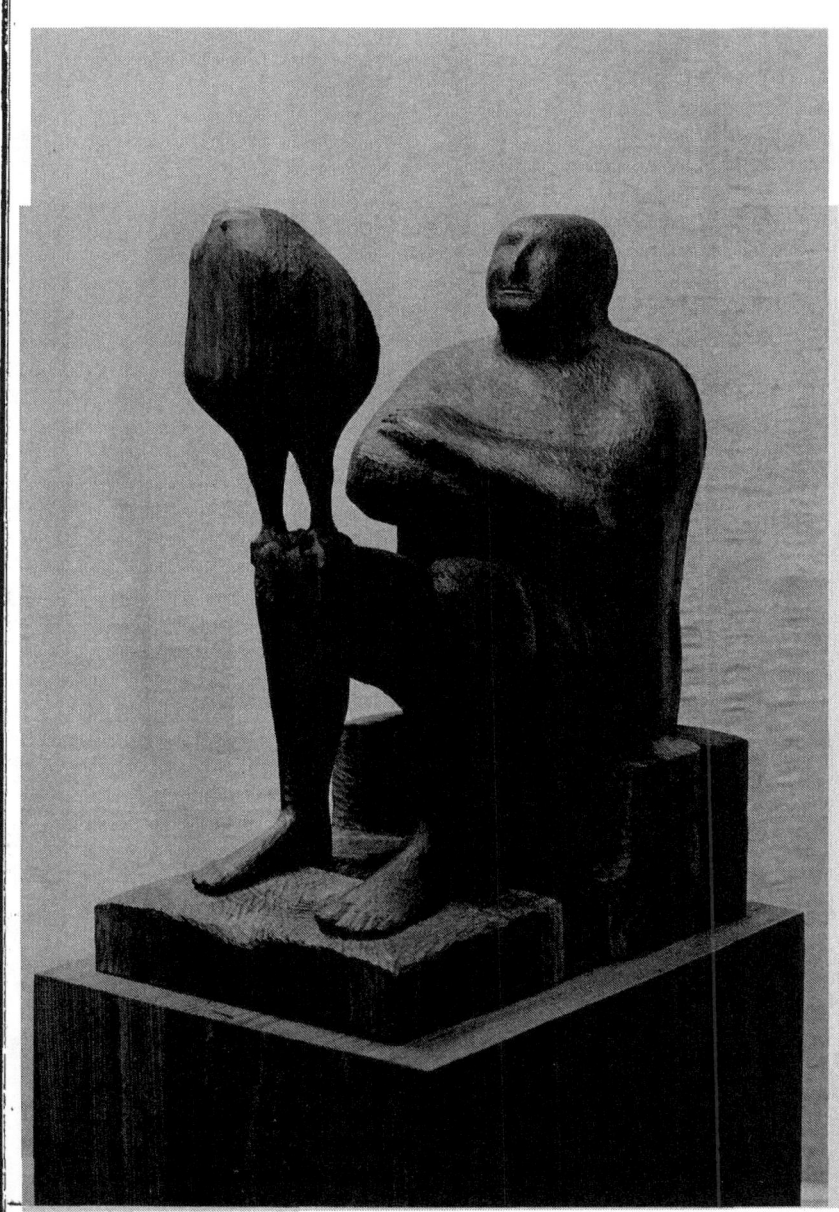

23. MAN WITH OWL, WALNUT, 1960

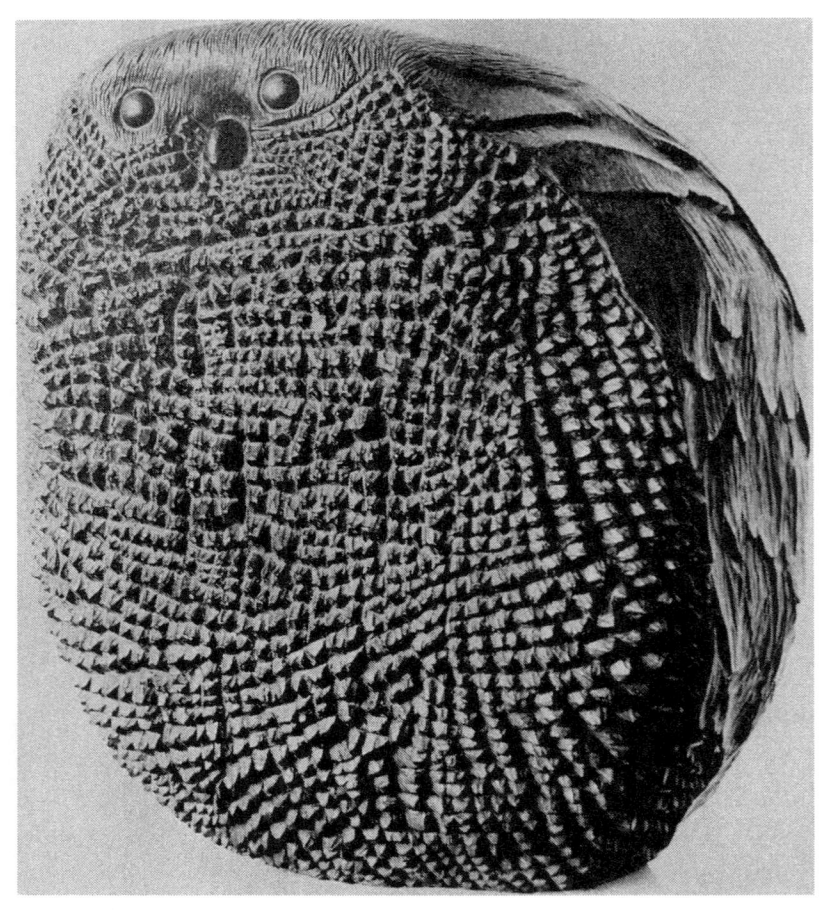

24. OWL, BRONZE, 1960

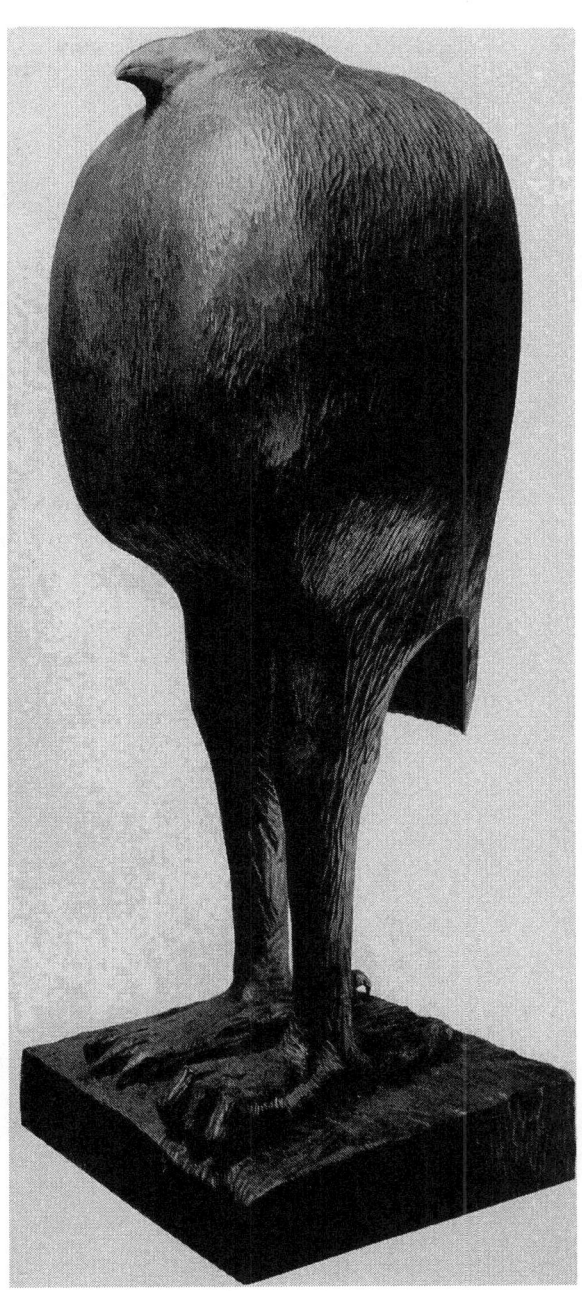

25. STANDING CROW, PINE, 1960

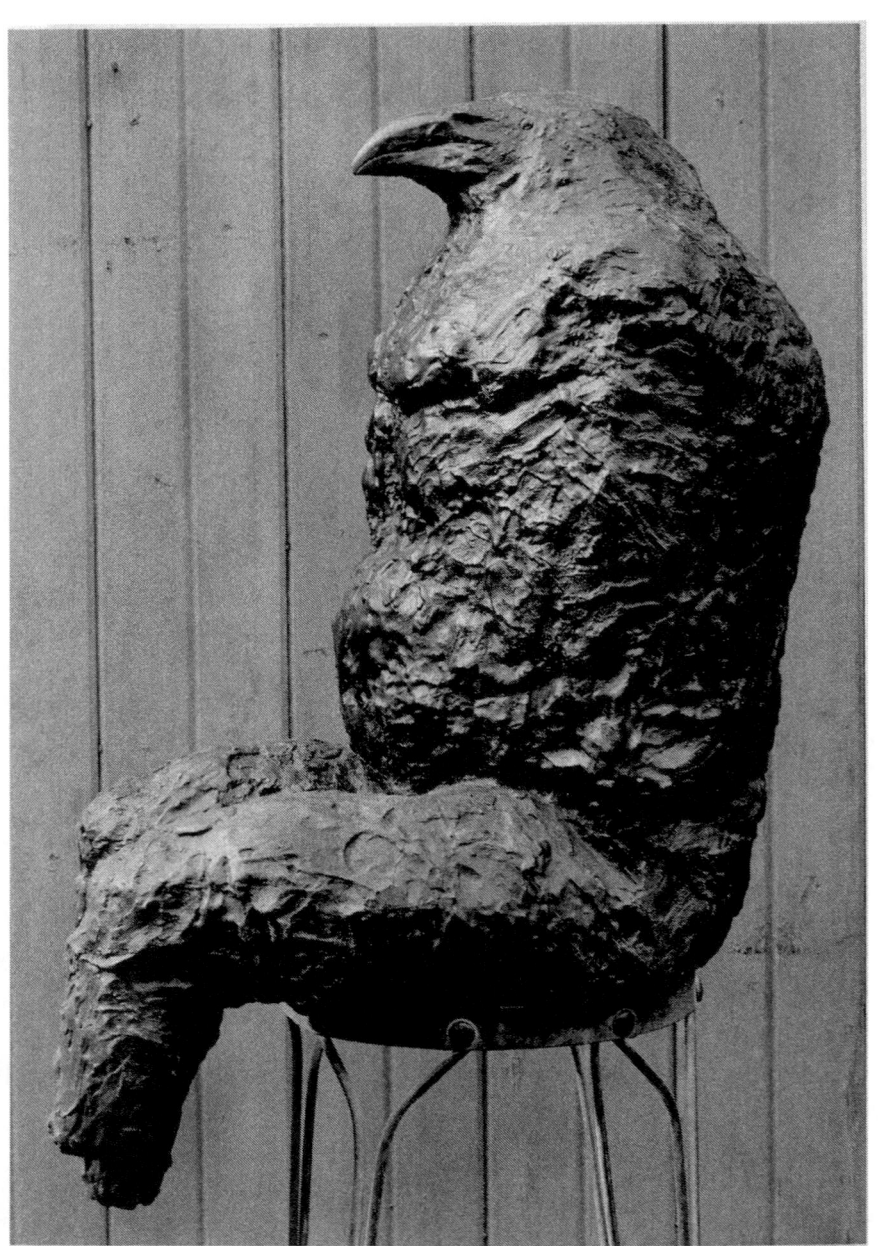

26. BIRDMAN, BRONZE, 1961

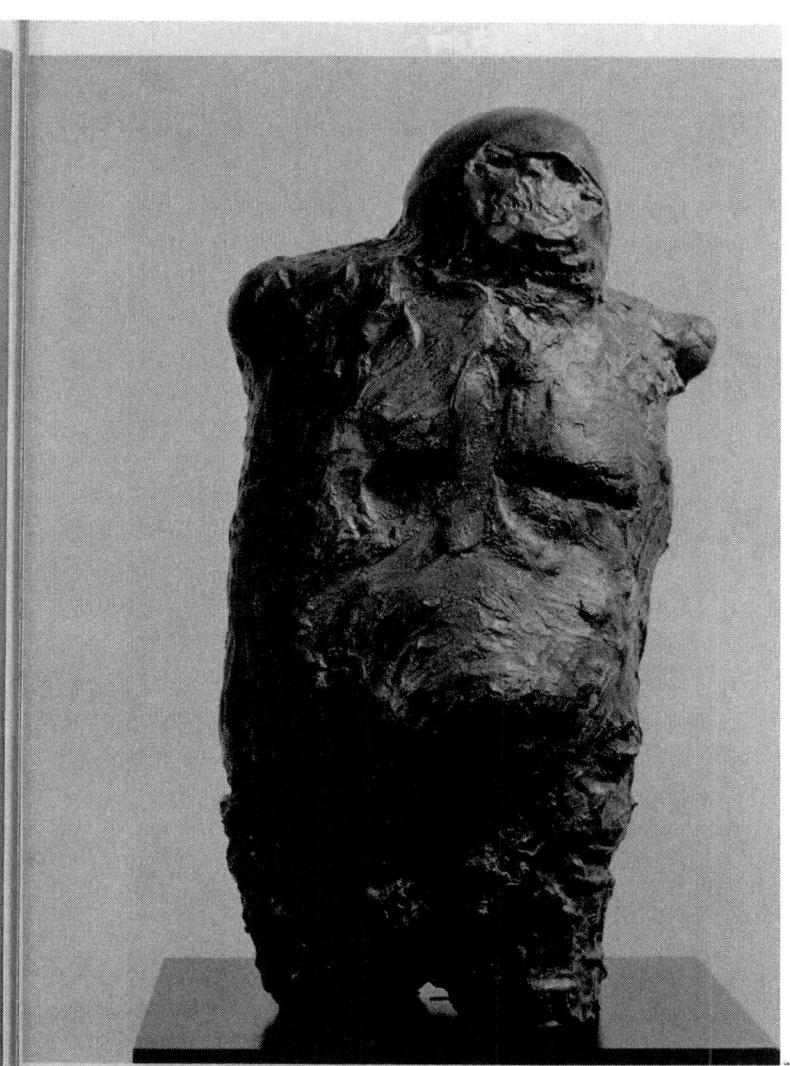

27. DEATH, BRONZE, 1961

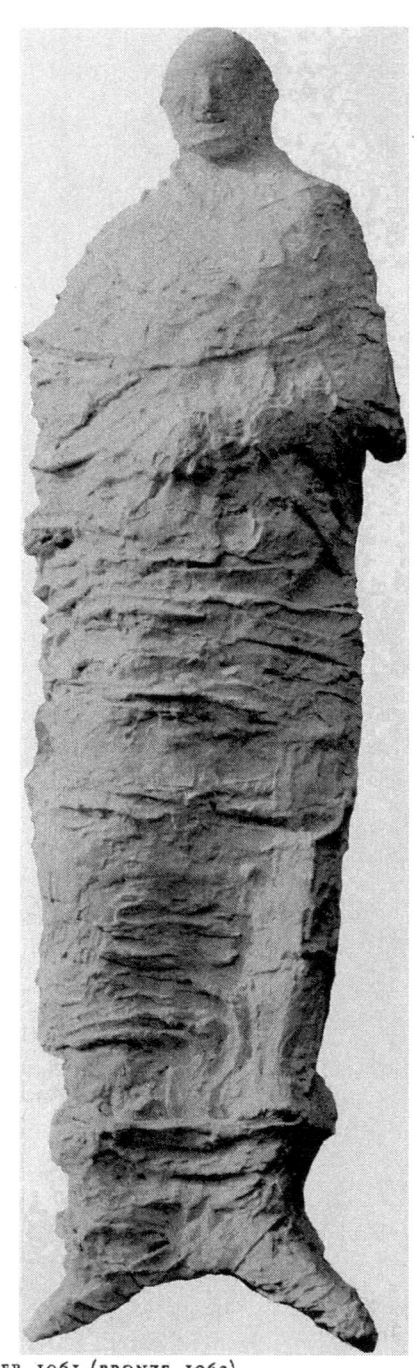

28. DEAD MAN, PLASTER, 1961 (BRONZE, 1962)

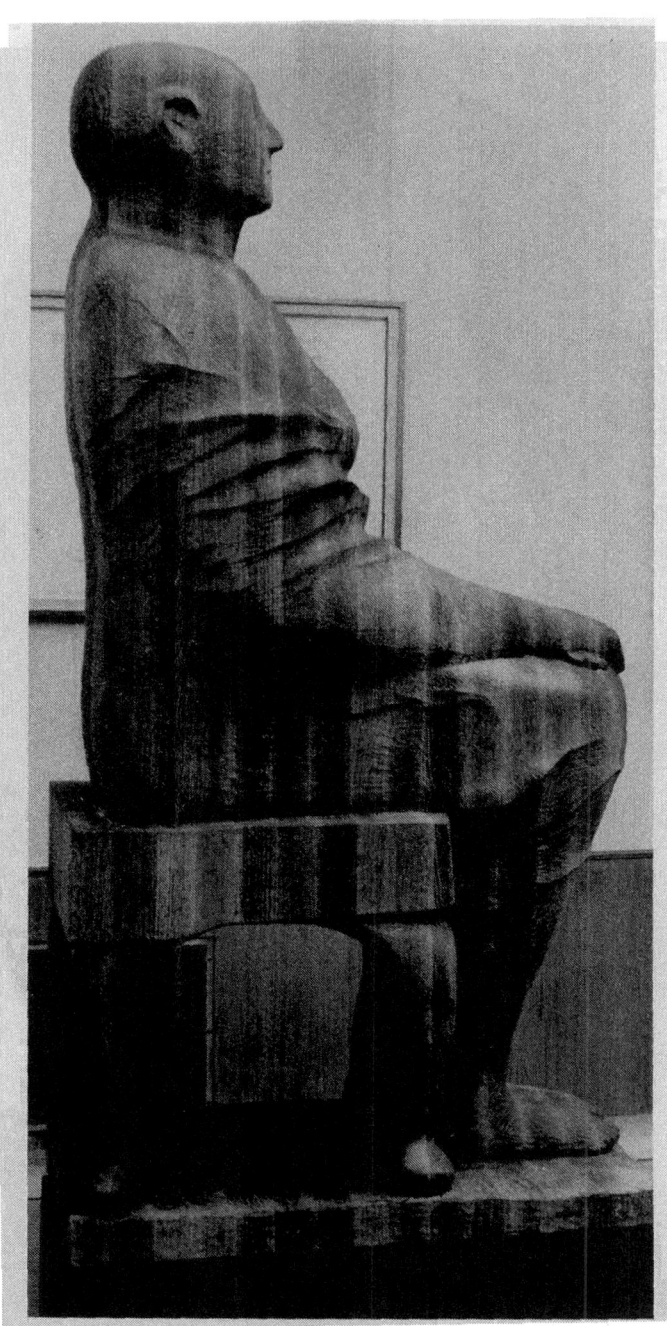

29. SEATED WOMAN, OAK, 1961

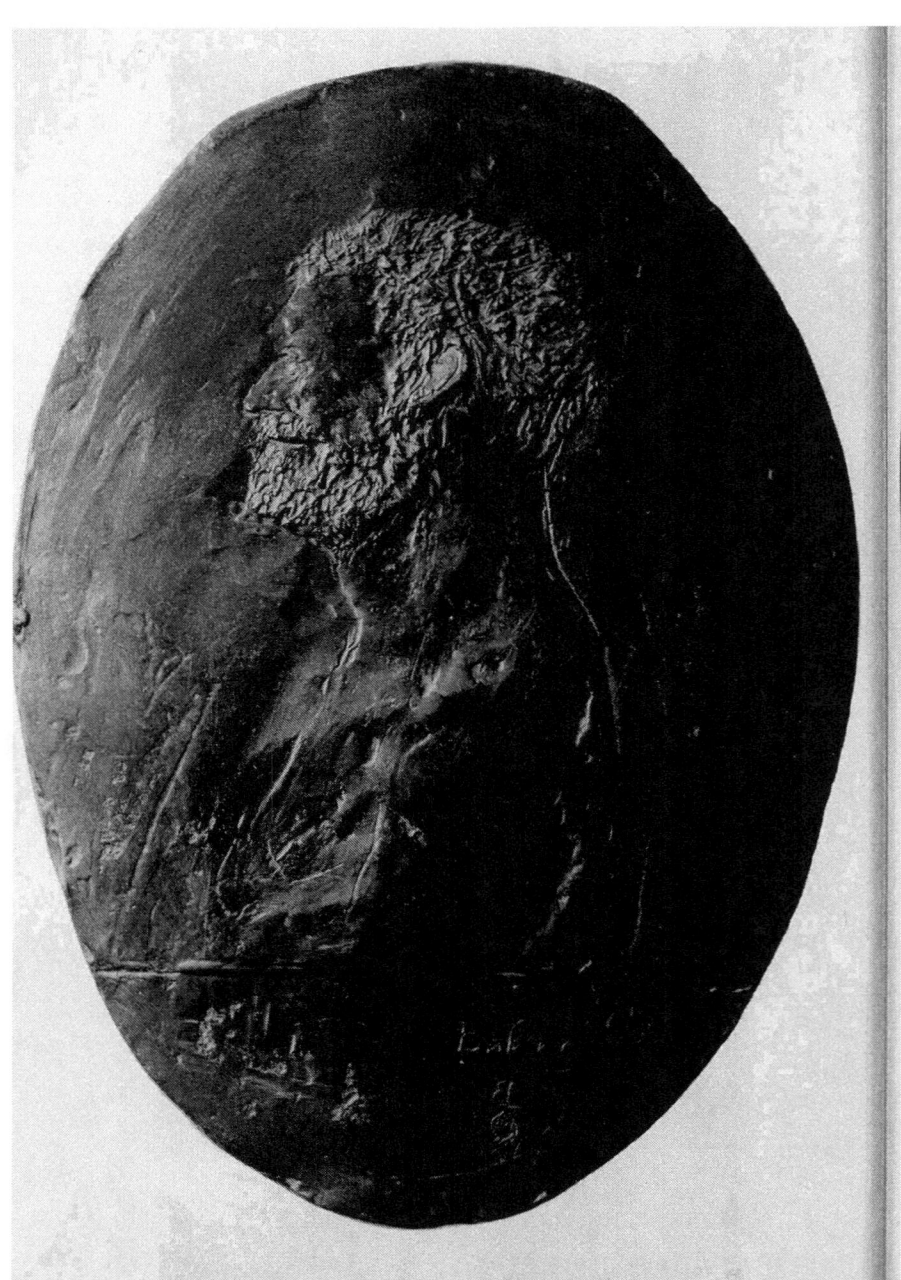

30. EAKINS, COPPER RELIEF, 1961

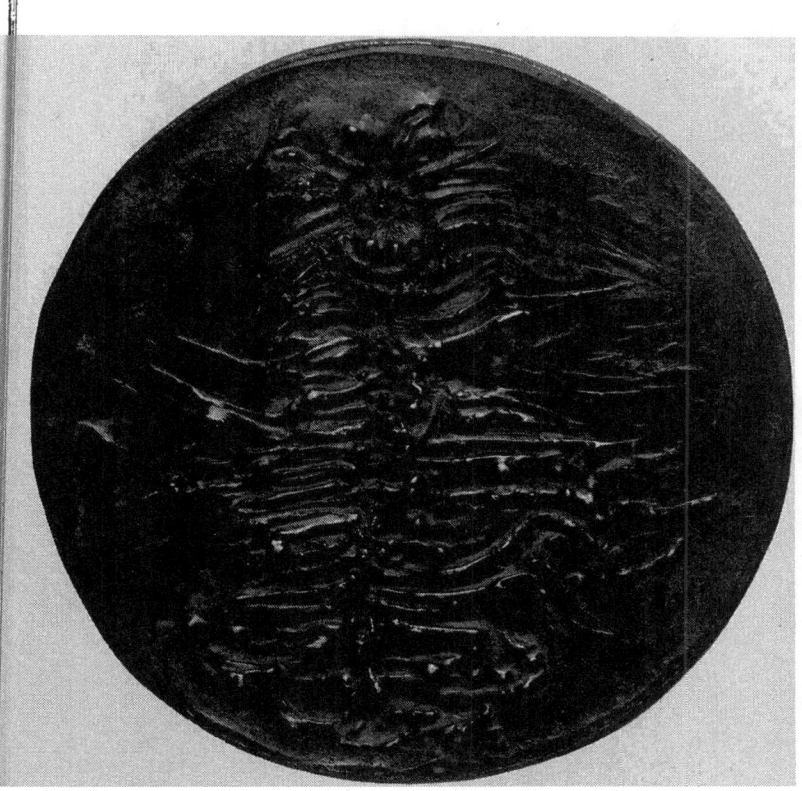

31. DENTATE ART NOUVEAU FLOWER, BRONZE RELIEF, 1961

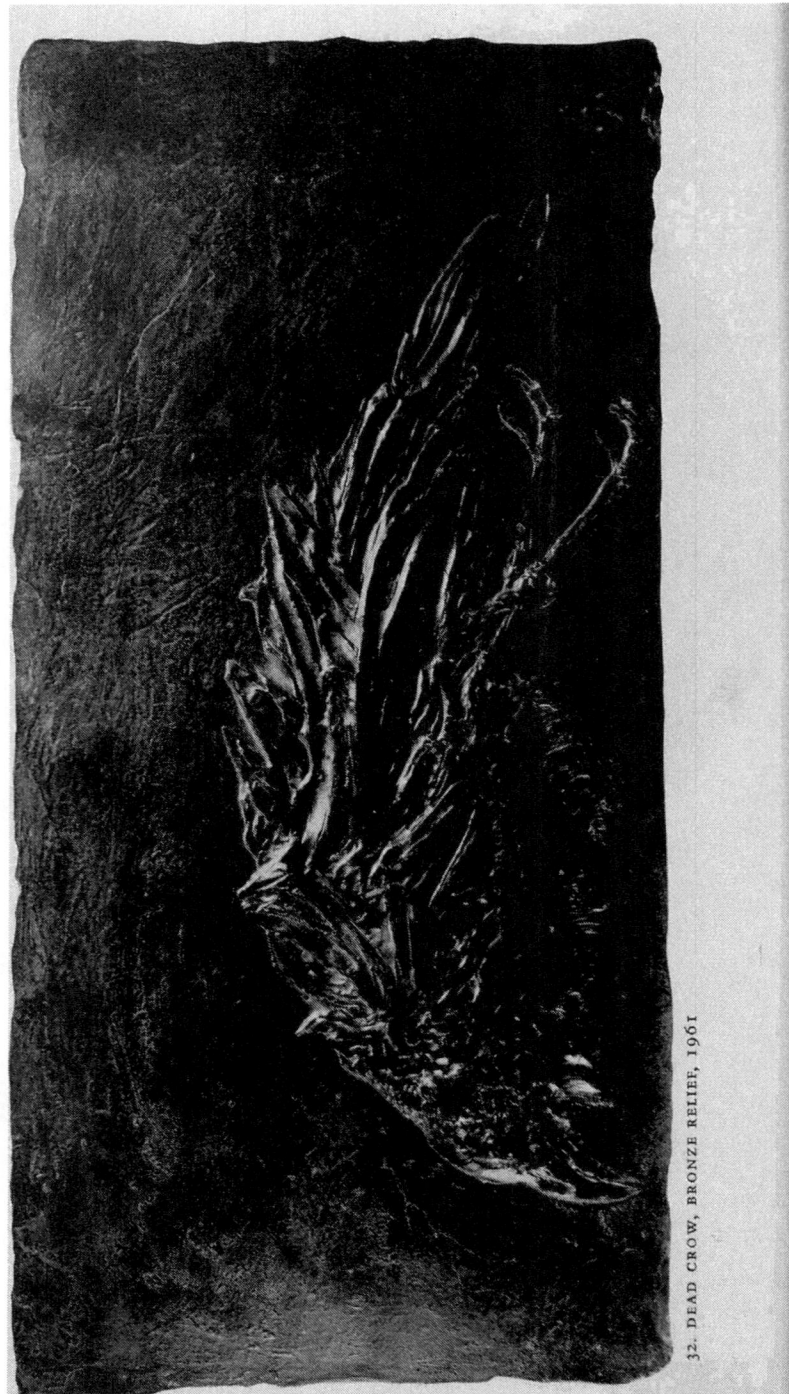

32. DEAD CROW, BRONZE RELIEF, 1961

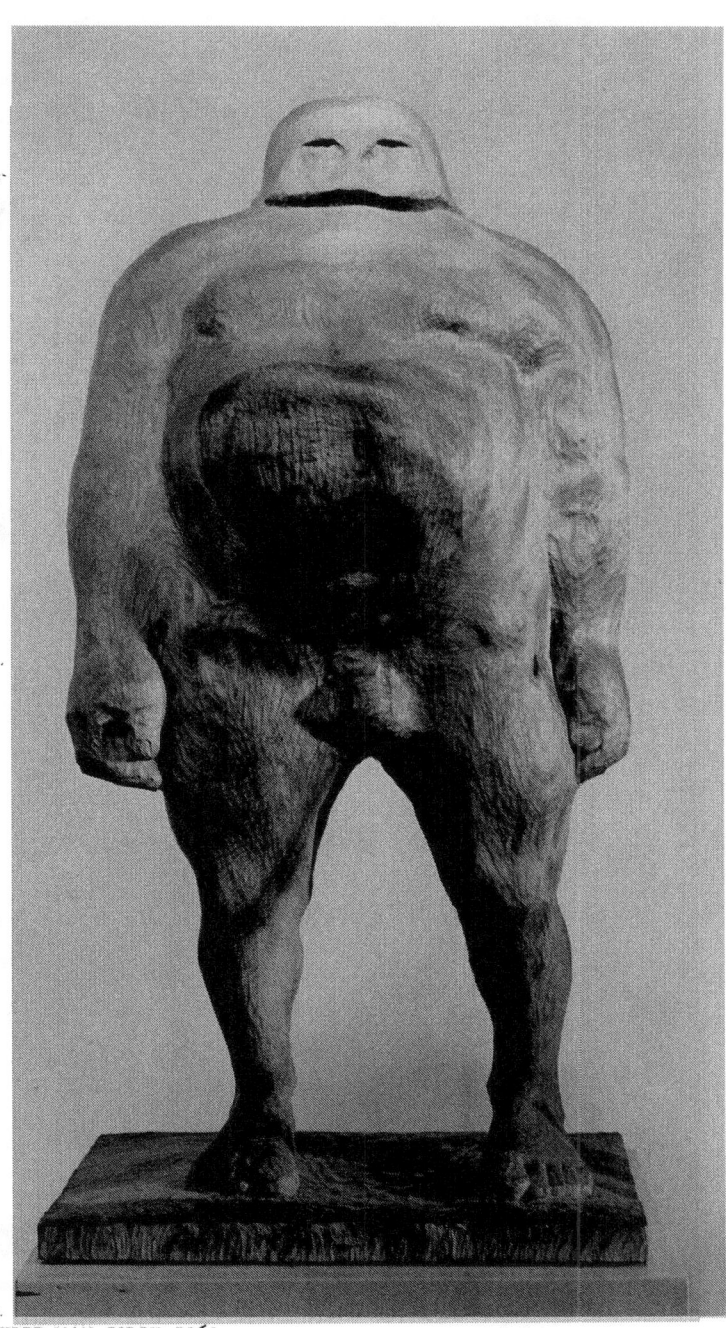

33. ARMOURED MAN, BIRCH, 1962

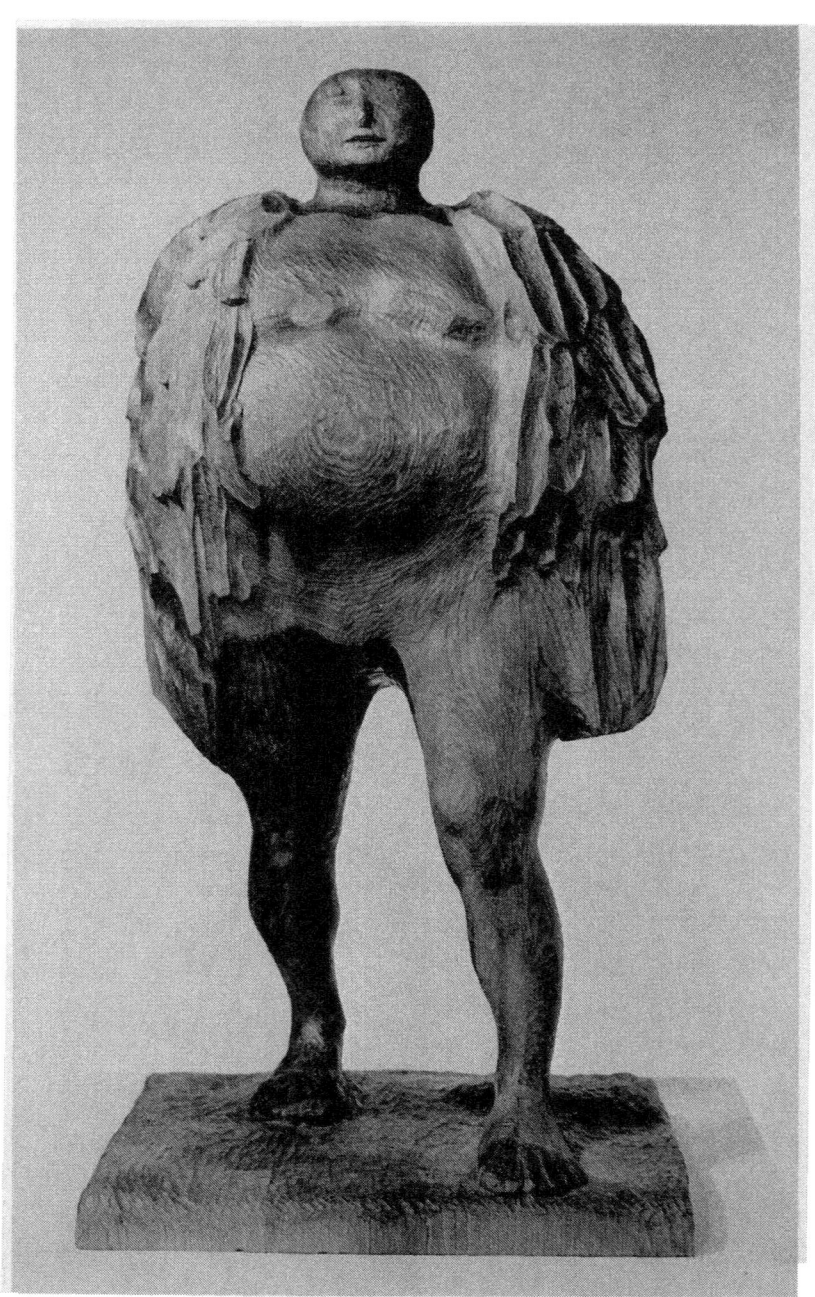

34. BENEVOLENT ANGEL, BIRCH, 1962

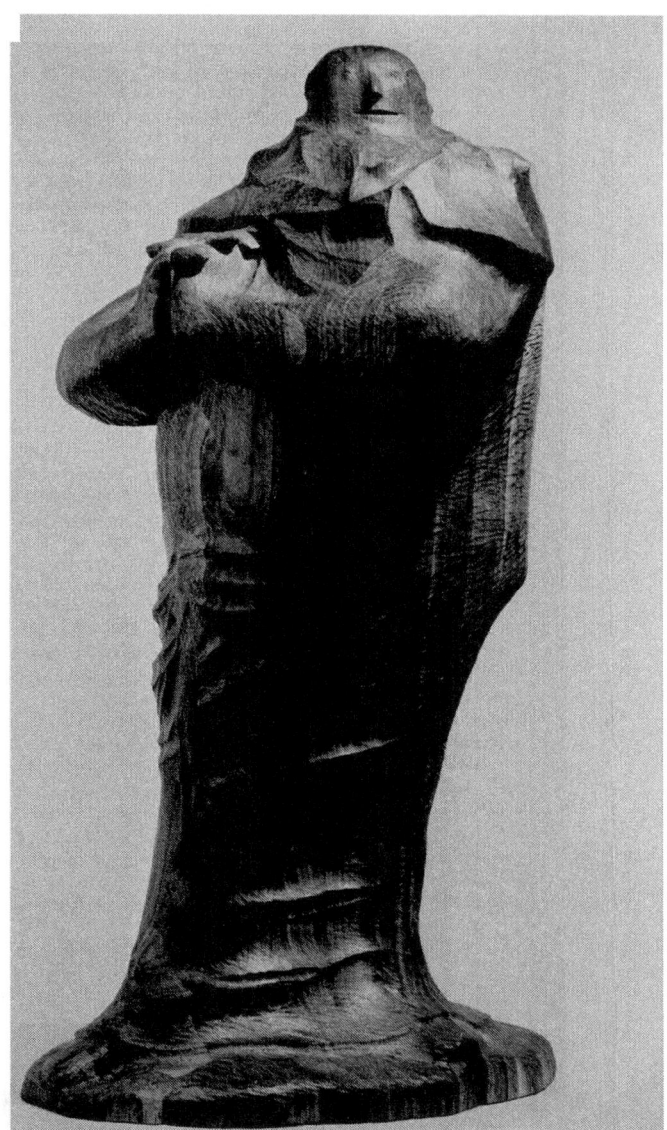

35. ST. THOMAS AQUINAS, WALNUT, 1962

DRAWINGS. At the risk of burying Caesar alive by praising him, I must say a few words about Leonard Baskin from the point of view of a fellow-collector of drawings who is interested in techniques, and who has been a fellow-collector of pots. Baskin first came to my eye in one of the Brooklyn Museum's large annual print shows in which Una Johnson has, over the years, reminded us that (to whatever stylish or unstylish category the printmaker's product will belong) planning, persistent craftsmanship, mental and physical labor are still ingredients of the arts. Soon afterwards I began to see Baskin's sculptures and drawings, and to know his types. ❧ It is practically impossible to disentangle the artist in his case from the learned man, the disciplined but witty humanist, and the craftsman, just as it is almost impossible to disentangle the sculptor from the draftsman from the printer and printmaker. What he seems to me to have done is to use everything that was delivered to him, to transform it by a private sort of incubation, and to return it to us consumers of works of art not exhausted, not made easy, but seasoned. This is eclecticism at its best (and eclecticism is not a bad word with me). ❧ The artist's house and his work-place are obviously revealing. I have seen a painter's dwelling that was rather like a funeral parlor; I have seen (happily) others that were hit-or-miss and 'lived in', even untroubled by problems of taste. I have known studios that were like elegant laboratories, and others more like the average layman's basement. Baskin's working-places are marked by the need to share with students: hence full of signs of work in progress, but with a sense of reticence, of a need for elbow-room for the neighbor as well as for himself. His house is the house of a person of substance who does not have to have conventional fleshpots, but who has exercised choices upon everything around him. There are indeed a great many things, but none is there by accident: very good rugs; broad tables; well-chosen, well-matted, well-framed drawings old and new; prints; bronze medallions; books by the hundreds. No nonsense about the simple life, but all in good order and system and pleasant sense: the scroddleware and creamware on upper shelves, the soft place below to lay down the Pisanello medals; the books are about drawing and drawings, or calligraphy, or printer's type specimens; or they are fine printing of the fifteenth, sixteenth, and seventeenth centuries, chiefly illustrated books; or illustrated children's classics or handsome bindings. ❧ All this, and all his other sources of knowledge, have contributed to the artist's drawings. He is not disposed to jettison, in romantic fashion, what he has learned. ❧ I don't know what sort of materials Baskin used before he became commercially successful, but I suspect that they were always as good as he could find. He uses many sorts of excellent papers, brushes from various parts of the world, assorted pens, a pointed pencil. All these are used freely but not spendthriftily. His knowledge of the many faces of older art, of mythology, and of morphology is considerable. But he is not engaged, like some designers for in-group advertising, in recreating old quaintnesses, the chap-book style, or desirable splendors. He seems rather to be getting and giving the advantage of ancient and recent wisdoms. By the same token, he is not a bit interested in pleasing anyone with superficial beauties; even those drawings of his which are easiest to take will be found full of thorny passages. His art seems to me to be very little for art's sake and very much an art to conceal art. When a tech-nique is above reproach, there is probably little need to mention it, but Baskin's methods are so interesting that some features must be mentioned. ✌ Every sheet of 'laid' or ridged paper has two scales: that of its own gross dimensions, seen at a glance, and that of its web of ridges, seen in blank only if one tips the sheet obliquely to a raking light, or seen normally when crayon or half-dry brush hits the high spots, leaves the valleys white, and so brings out the corduroy-like texture. On such paper, Baskin usually draws with a brush, a brush used in the big figures rather stabbingly and often apparently at arm's length, but as often with an upward motion as downwards or sweeping around. He can also use the point of a Japanese writer's brush, or a broad wash-brush full of diluted ink. When he wants a 'grey' or half-tone other than that of dilution, he does not always rely on the crumbly tex-ture produced by the half-dry brush and the grain of the paper; he will take a pen and draw fine sub-systems of lines which, by the intervals between them, are scaled to the parallel ridges of the paper though they may cut across them. Many of the drawings of grasses, flowers, and teasels have skeletons of broad-brush sweeping lines, sometimes in brown as well as black, with the usual crumbles at the edges. At first sight one supposes that certain areas of speckle are also crumbles, but look-ing more carefully one discovers that they are elaborate fine-pen drawing, some-times radiating systems of petals, sometimes imbricated teasels, sometimes (in other sorts of subjects) specifications of feathers or beards or eye-wrinkles, creeping in or out of washes or larger networks. It is an experience a little like going 'through the looking-glass' to penetrate such a drawing. The *Owl* in this exhibition is peculiarly rich in its mixture of wash, point of the brush, and pen. ✌ In his figure drawings, as in his sculpture and woodcuts, Baskin makes capital use of some good old devices for forcing scale: the tiny head or spindly legs that gigantize the body, the piglike concentration of features in a huge bland face. His angels (not sexless, not elegant) and his bird-headed men and other such mythologies are some of the best vehicles of that sense, which pervades all his work, of the inconsistency of humanity, its cruelty and ridiculousness, its pomposity and panic, its heroism. The death that always inhabits the body, whether its victory be complete or not, is also pervasive. Not Death as a Friend or Death as an Enemy, but death as an opposite number; in this, as in many other aspects of his continuance of long tradition, there is a feeling of continuum itself, of the pre-Renaissance disregard of the precious individual. Yet Baskin has personal heroes. He does not, however, idealize representatives of a race to whose improvement he may look forward, any more than Aldous Huxley idealizes present human beings about whose posterity he is optimistic. ❧ In the recent series of drawings for Homer, Baskin has found few heroes without some gross giveaway of flaws that Flaxman guarded. Baskin would rather Homer's personages had been less cruel, but he has pulled no punches in drawing his idea of them. At about the same time as this series, presumably commissioned, he produced a different series for relaxation: fantasies out of the seventeenth century, Theophrastic 'characters' perhaps, a young Rembrandt, a Guercinesque dandy, an obvious rogue, a French-looking politician. They are rather like the kind of visual jokes that Max Beerbohm and Edward Lear did on their contemporaries, but with something of the sense of the past that made T. M. Cleland's antiquarian decorations so spirited: they are enormous fun whether you are in the know of the parodies or not. There are, of course, reminiscences of other artists, Blake, Goya, Dürer, more recently Tchelitchew and Bacon and Rivers; all of which is not to complain of but to be thankful for. I for one am pleased to discover that Ben Shahn and Rico Lebrun are admired by Leonard Baskin. I trust my own pleasure in 'reading' Baskin's work at leisure will not rob any visitor to this exhibition of the first shock of pleasure at sight.

WINSLOW AMES

DRAWINGS

1.
PSEUDO-SUICIDE OF
HIPPOLYTE BAYARD
Ink, 1954, 15 ⅝ × 20 ⅜ ins.
Mr. Nathan Chaiken
New York

2.
STUDY FOR THE PORTRAIT
OF WILLIAM BLAKE
Ink, 1955, 13 × 20
Mr. Jay C. Leff
Uniontown, Pennsylvania

3.
HEAD OF BLAKE
Ink, 1956, 30½ × 22
Mr. Jay C. Leff
Uniontown, Pennsylvania

4.
TORMENTED MAN
Ink and wash, 1956, 39½ × 26½
Whitney Museum of American Art
(Living Arts Foundation Fund)
New York

5.
KITE AND DOG
Ink, pencil, and red crayon, 1957,
31 × 22½
Mr. Charles Gwathmey
New York

6.
OWL
Ink and colored wash, 1957, 24¼ × 30½
Mrs. G. Macculloch Miller
New York

7.
AFTER MANTEGNA
Ink and wash, 1957, 39 × 26
Mr. and Mrs. Sidney Kingsley
New York

8.
GRIEVING ANGEL
Ink, 1957, 22 × 30½
The Joseph H. Hirshhorn Collection
New York

9.
WINTER WEEDS
Ink, 1957, 32 ¼ × 30 ⅝
Mrs. Leonard Baskin
Northampton, Massachusetts

10.
THE GREAT TEASEL
Ink, 1957, 22 ¼ × 31
Mr. Jay C. Leff
Uniontown, Pennsylvania

11.
BOUQUET
Ink and wash, 1958, 21 ¾ × 30 ⅜
Mr. and Mrs. Winslow Ames
Saunderstown, Rhode Island

12.
FLEA
Ink and colored wash, 1958, 22 ¼ × 30 ⅛
Private Collection
New York

13.
ANGEL OF DEATH
Ink and wash, 1958, 39 ¾ × 26 ⅝
Mrs. Leonard Baskin
Northampton, Massachusetts

14.
ANGEL OF DEATH
Ink and wash, 1958, 39 × 25 ½
Mr. Lee Nordness
New York

15.
BARTLEBY THE SCRIVENER
Ink, 1958, 22 ¼ × 30 ¼
Mr. Malcolm Goldstein
New York

16.
MARAT
Ink and wash, 1958, 40 × 27
Stephen and Sybil Stone Foundation
Newton Centre, Massachusetts

17.
CARL DREYER'S ST. JOAN
Ink, 1959, 22 ½ × 30
Mrs. Leonard Baskin
Northampton, Massachusetts

18.
GLUTTED DEATH
Ink and wash, 1959, 40 × 26
Mr. M. J. Stewart
Wilton, Connecticut

19.
DEAD CROW
Ink and wash, 1959, 26 × 40 ¼
Mr. William C. Esty
New York

20.
SEA BIRD
Ink and wash, 1960, 40 × 26
Grace Borgenicht Gallery
New York

21.
STUDY FOR JOB
Ink and wash, 1961, 18 ¼ × 22 ¾
Mrs. Katharine Kuh
New York

22.
REMBRANDT
Ink and wash, 1961, 41 ¼ × 29 ½
Mr. and Mrs. Lawrence Fleischman
Detroit, Michigan

23.
DUTCH ARTIST
Ink and wash, 1961, 22 ½ × 30 ¾
Dr. and Mrs. S. Lifschutz
New Brunswick, New Jersey

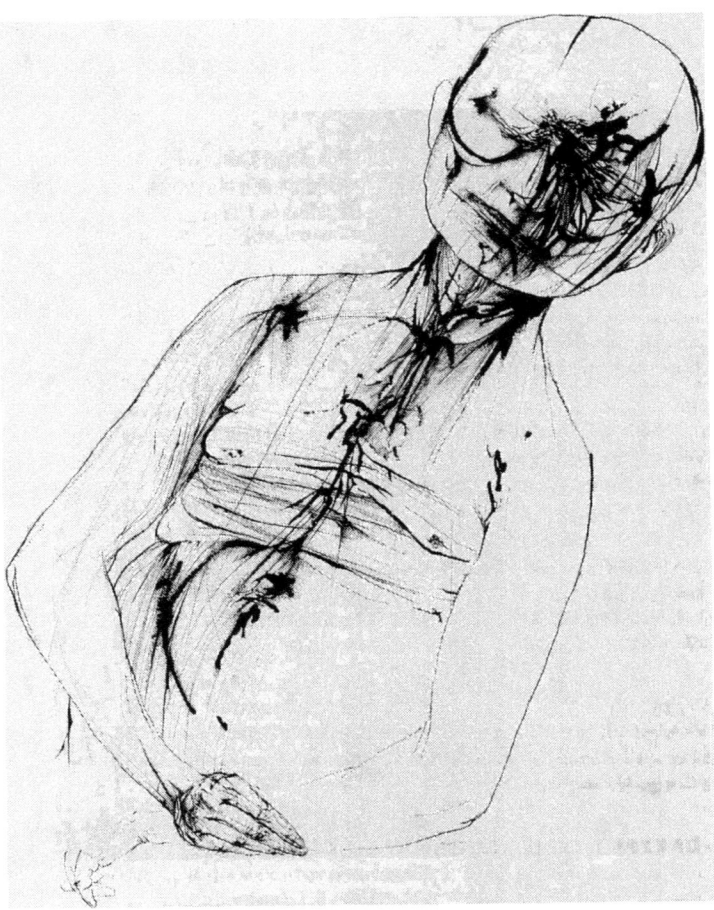

I. PSEUDO-SUICIDE OF HIPPOLYTE BAYARD, INK, 1954

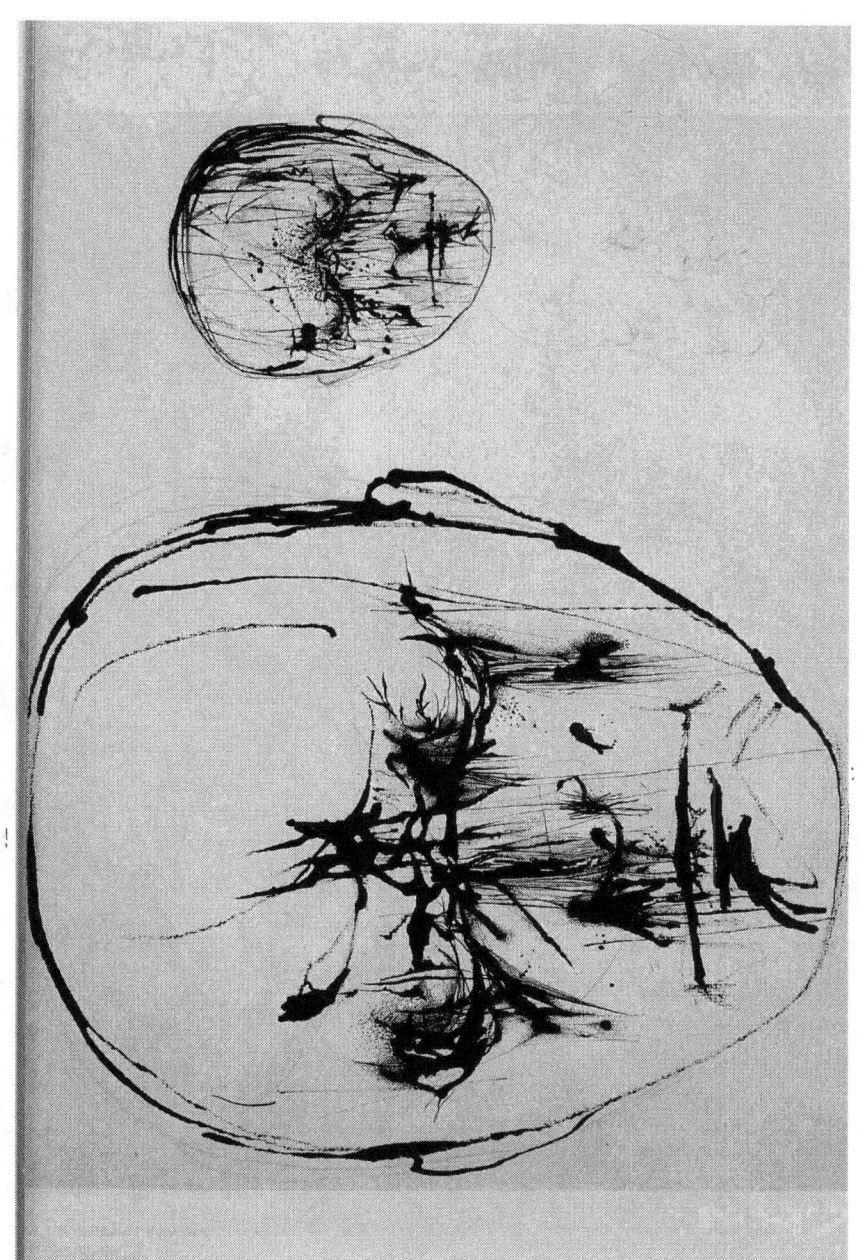

2. STUDY FOR THE PORTRAIT OF WILLIAM BLAKE, INK, 1955

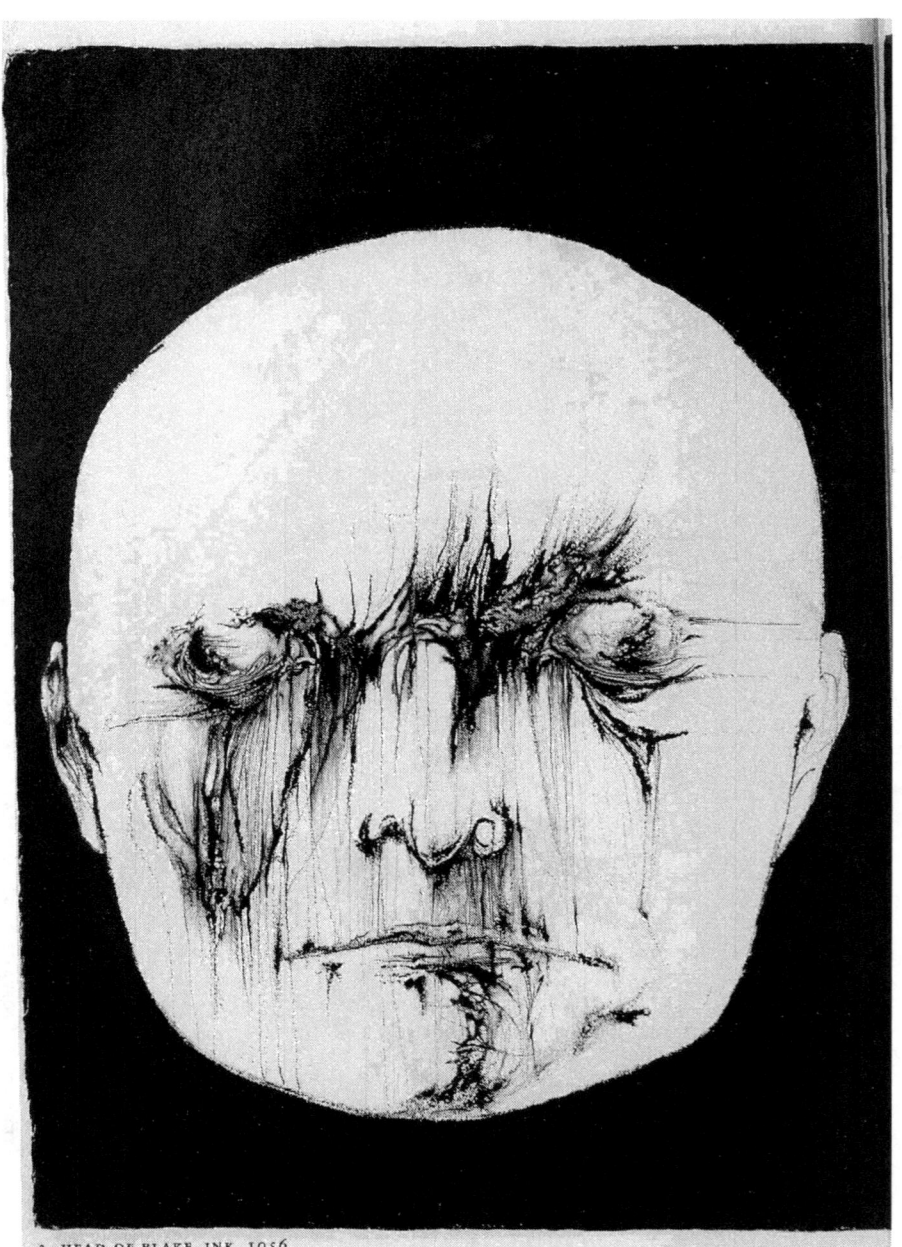

3. HEAD OF BLAKE, INK, 1956

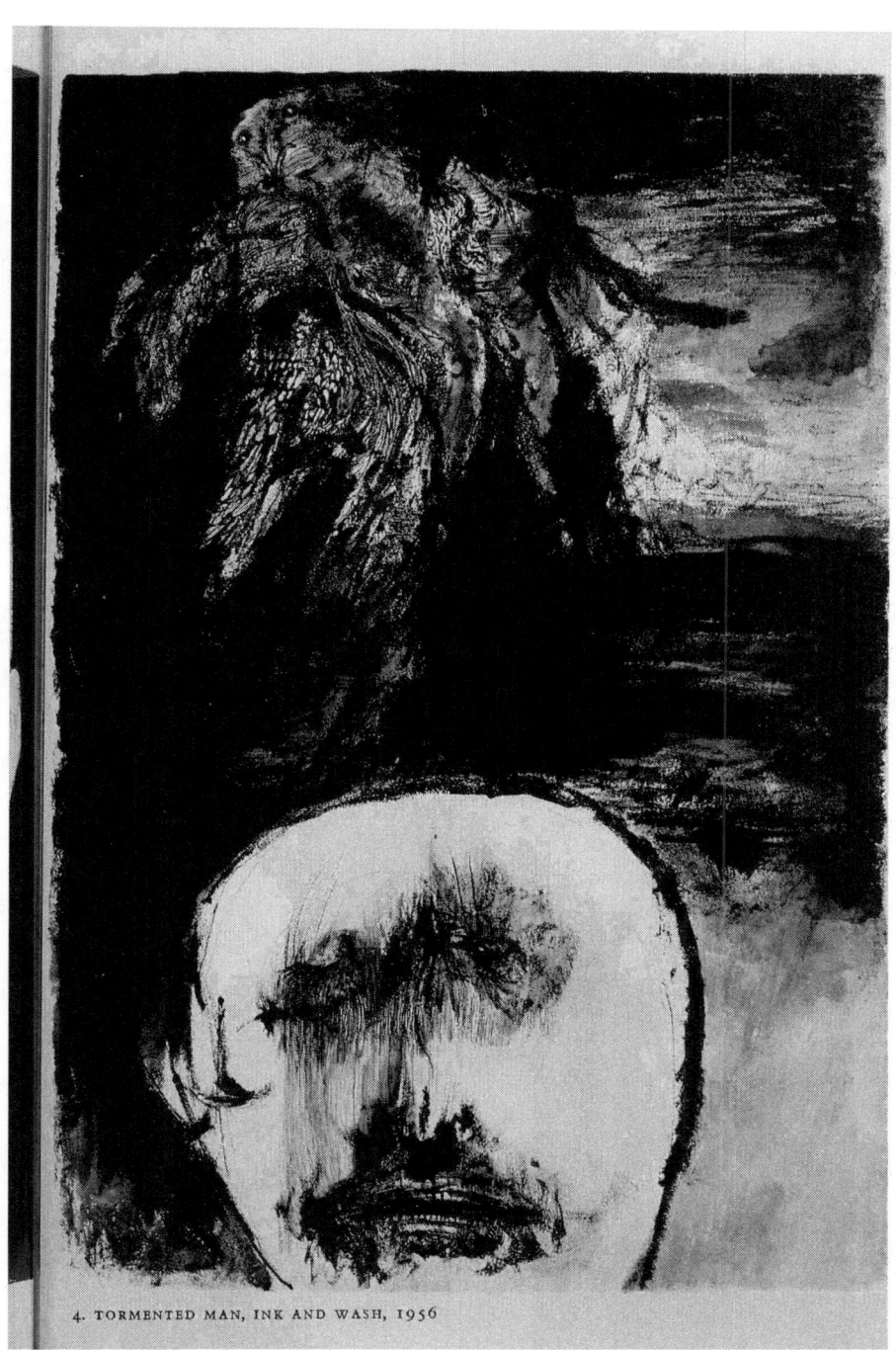

4. TORMENTED MAN, INK AND WASH, 1956

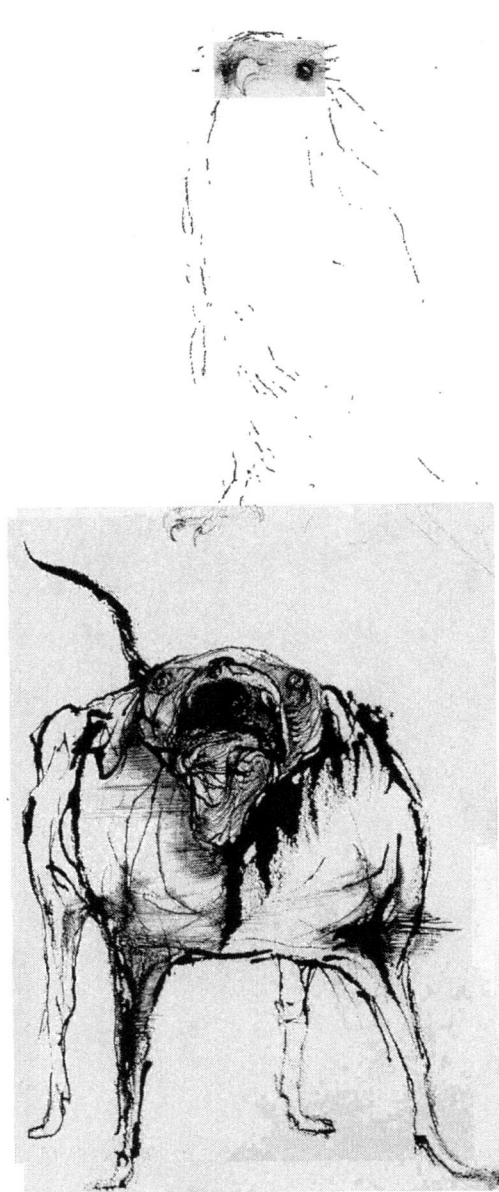

5. KITE AND DOG, INK, PENCIL, AND RED CRAYON, 1957

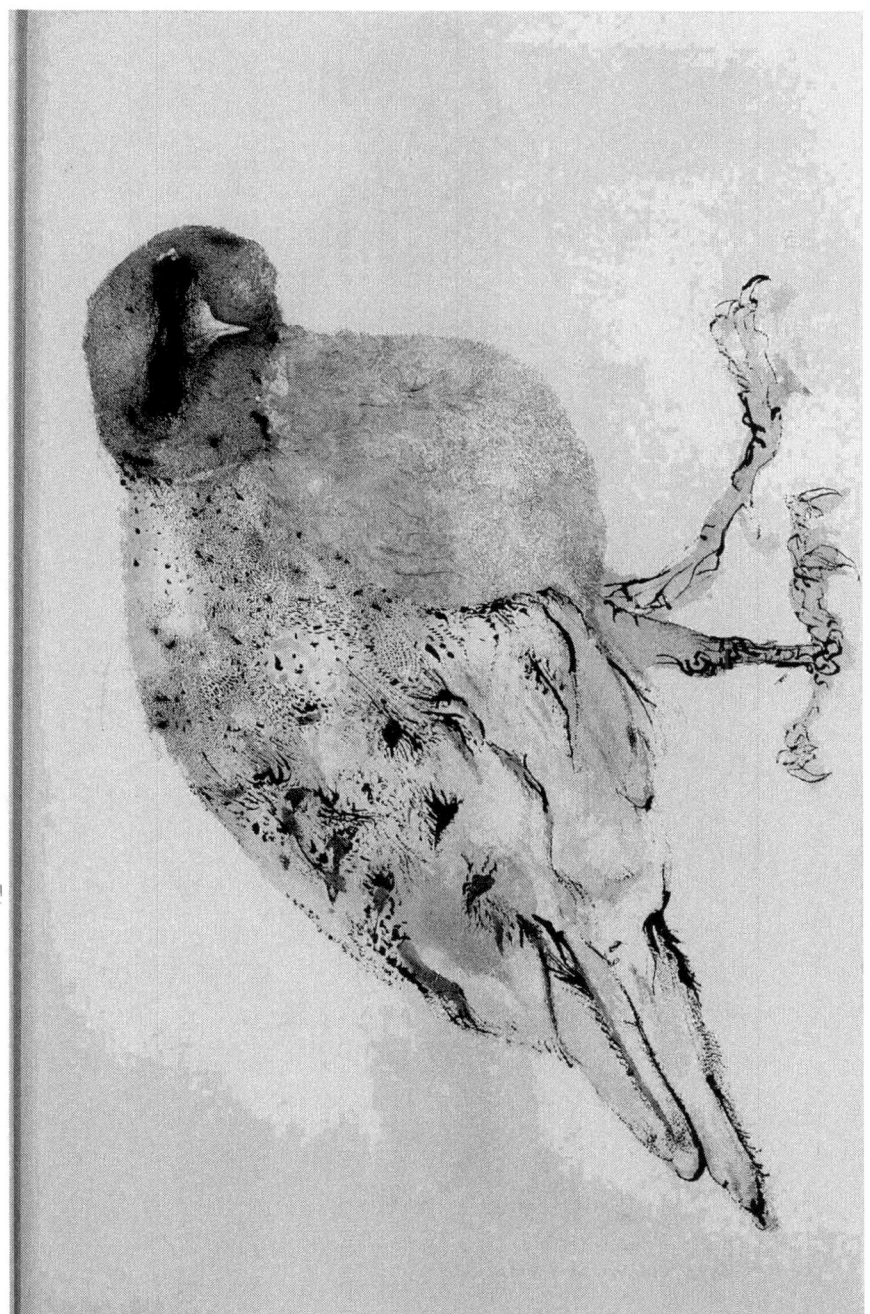

6. OWL, INK AND COLORED WASH, 1957

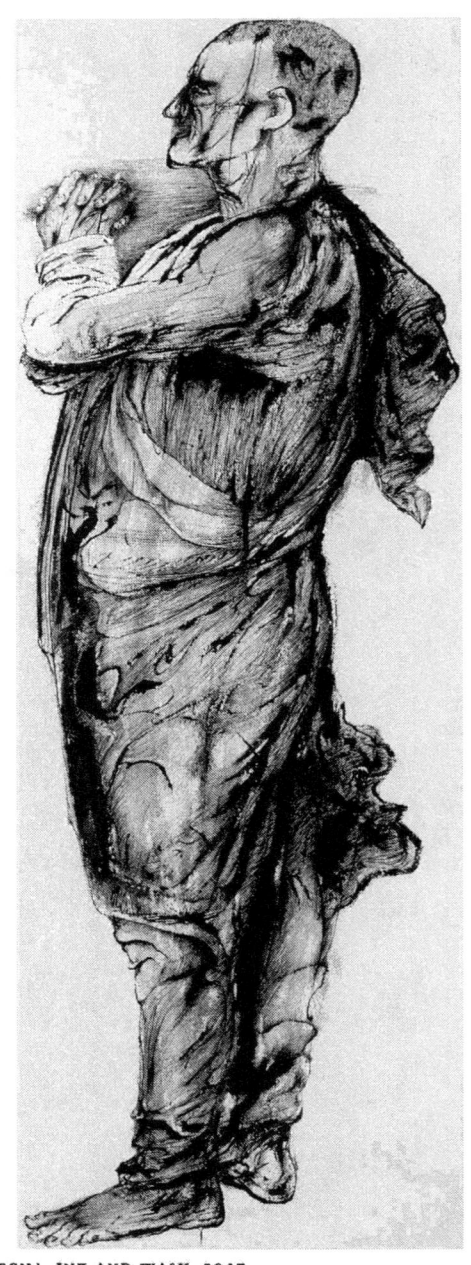

7. AFTER MANTEGNA, INK AND WASH, 1957

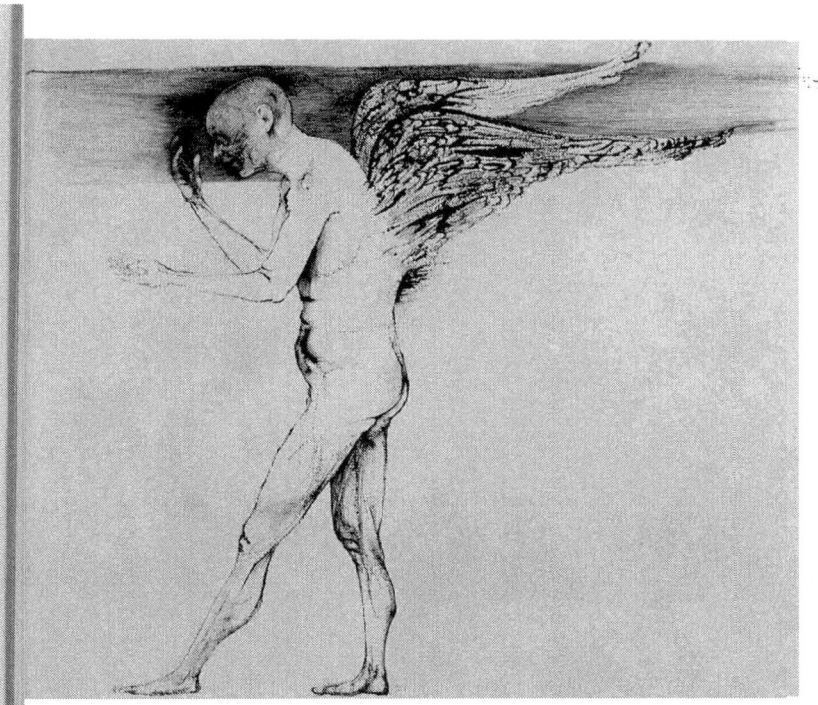

8. GRIEVING ANGEL, INK, 1957

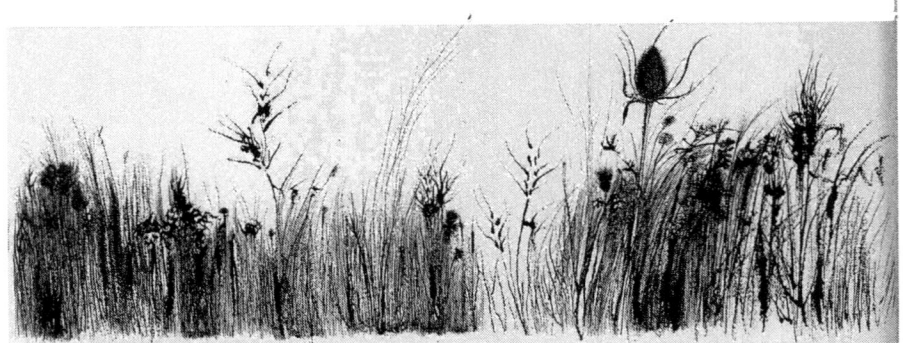

9. WINTER WEEDS, INK, 1957

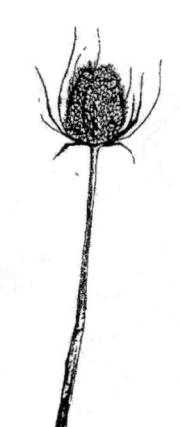

10. THE GREAT TEASEL, INK, 1957

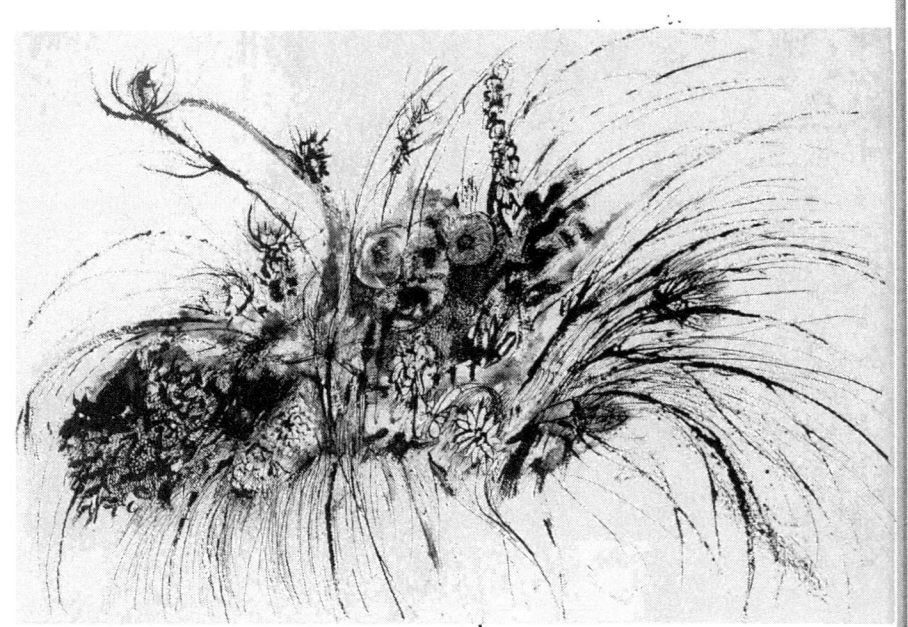

11. BOUQUET, INK AND WASH, 1958

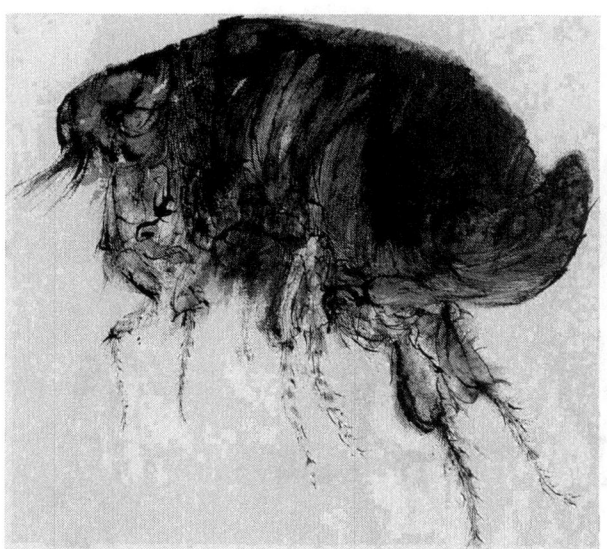

12. FLEA, INK AND COLORED WASH, 1958

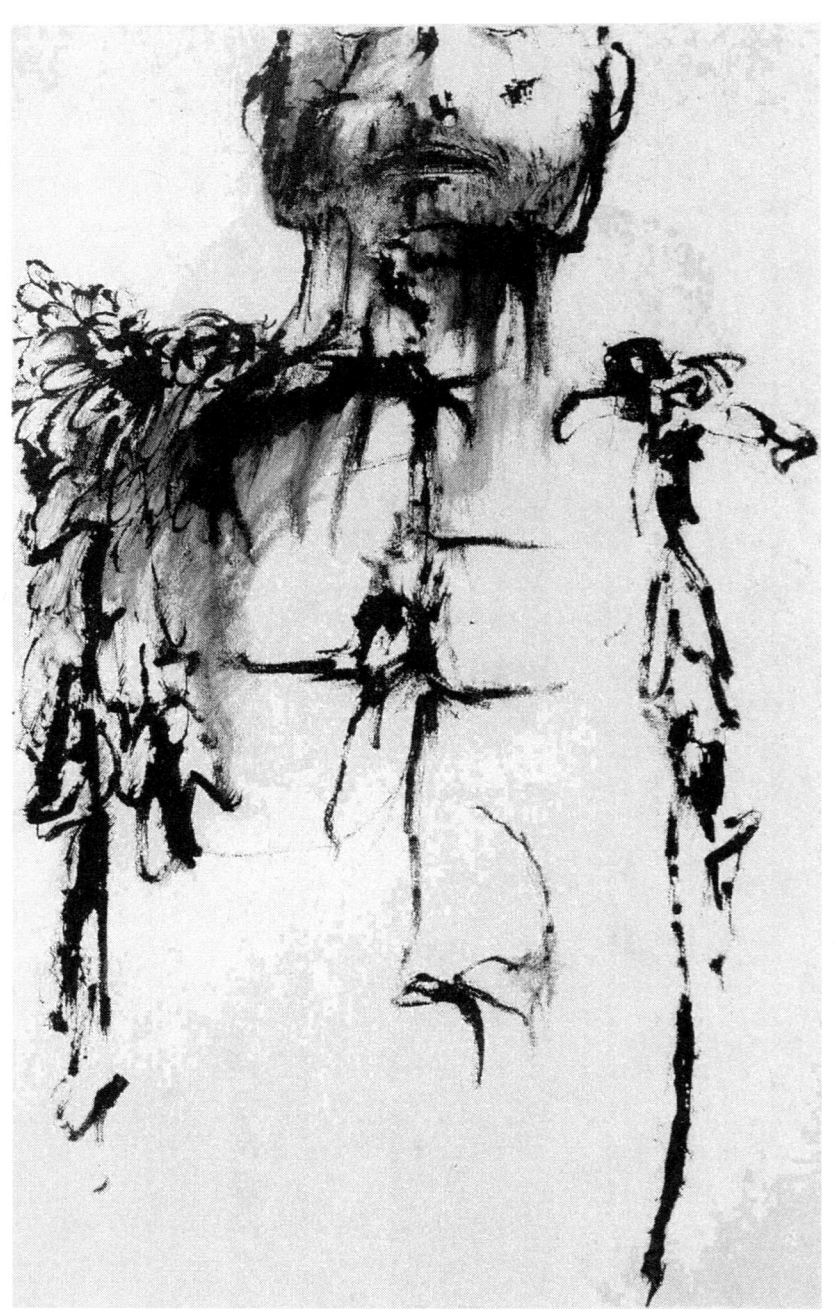

13. ANGEL OF DEATH, INK AND WASH, 1958

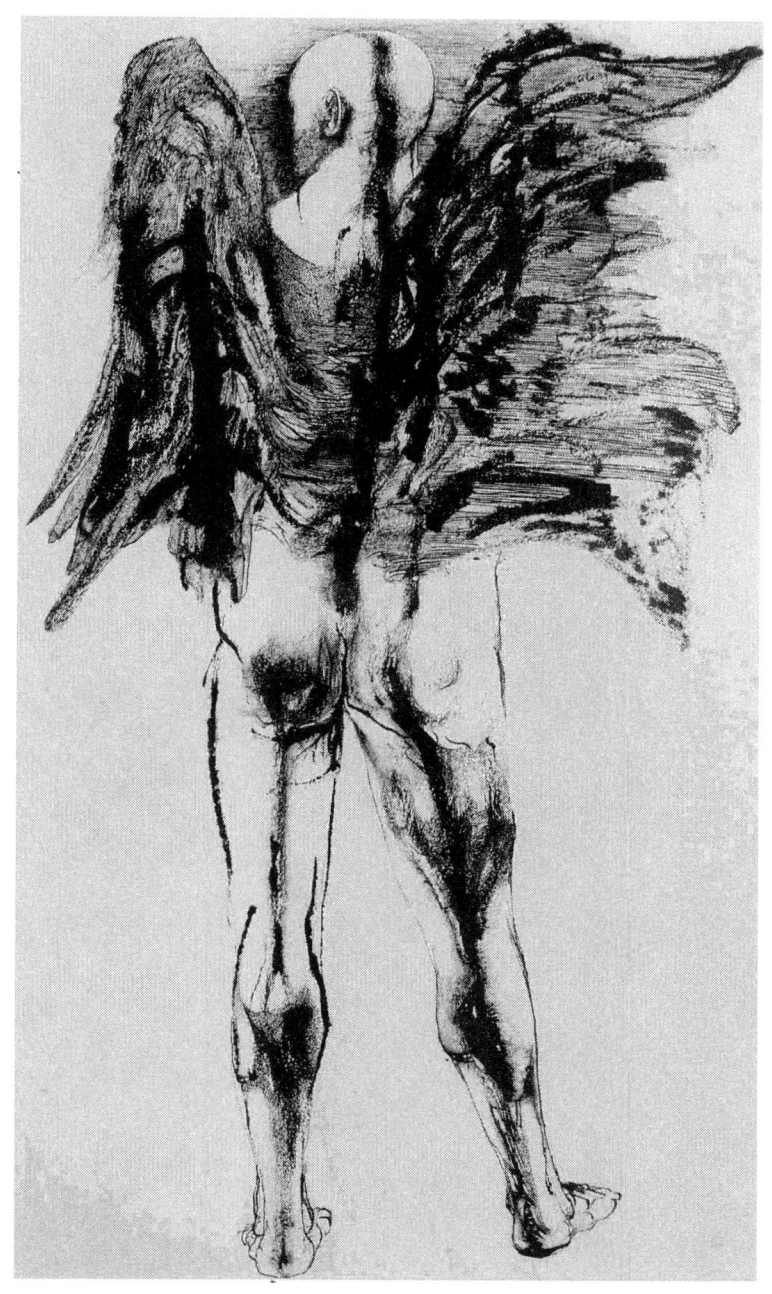

14. ANGEL OF DEATH, INK AND WASH, 1958

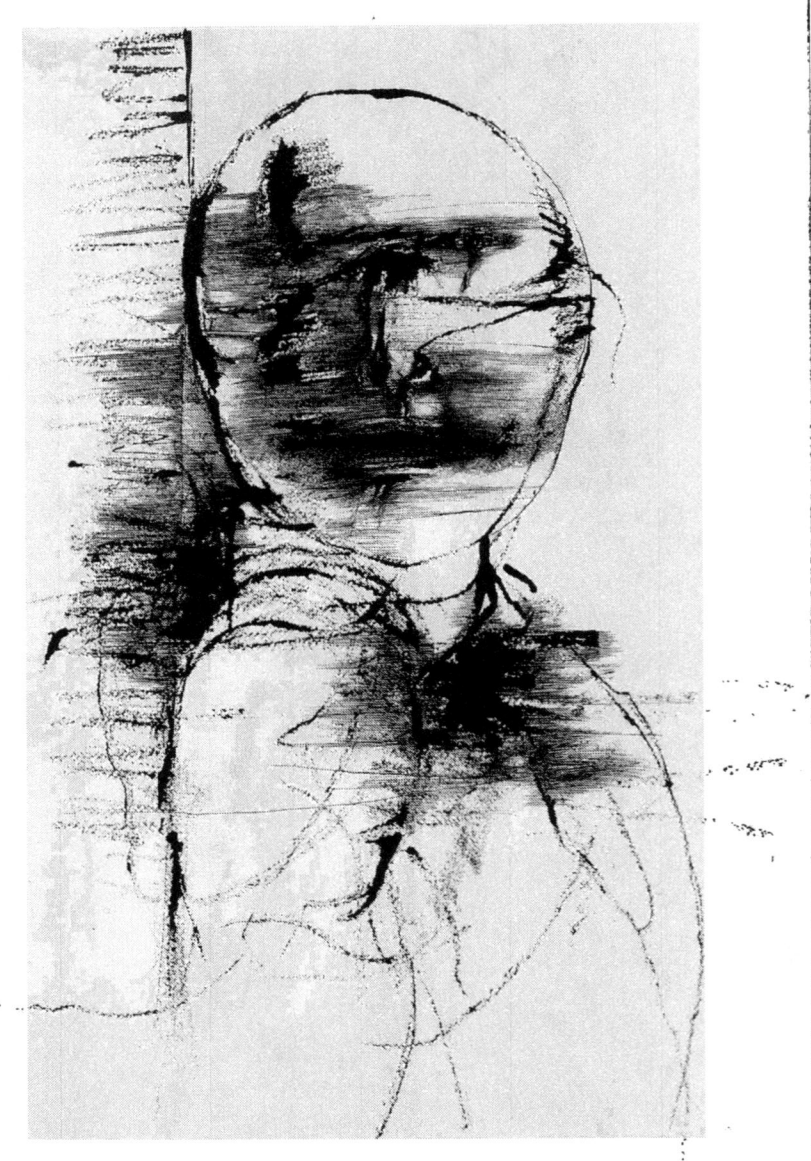

15. BARTLEBY THE SCRIVENER, INK, 1958

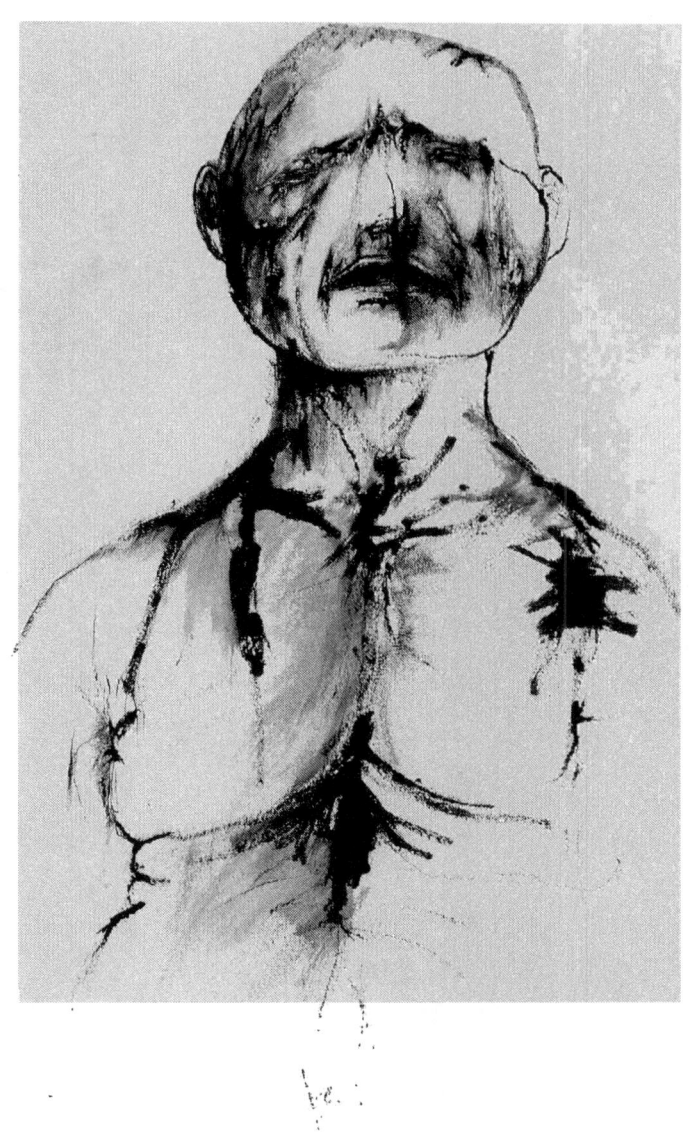

16. MARAT, INK AND WASH, 1958

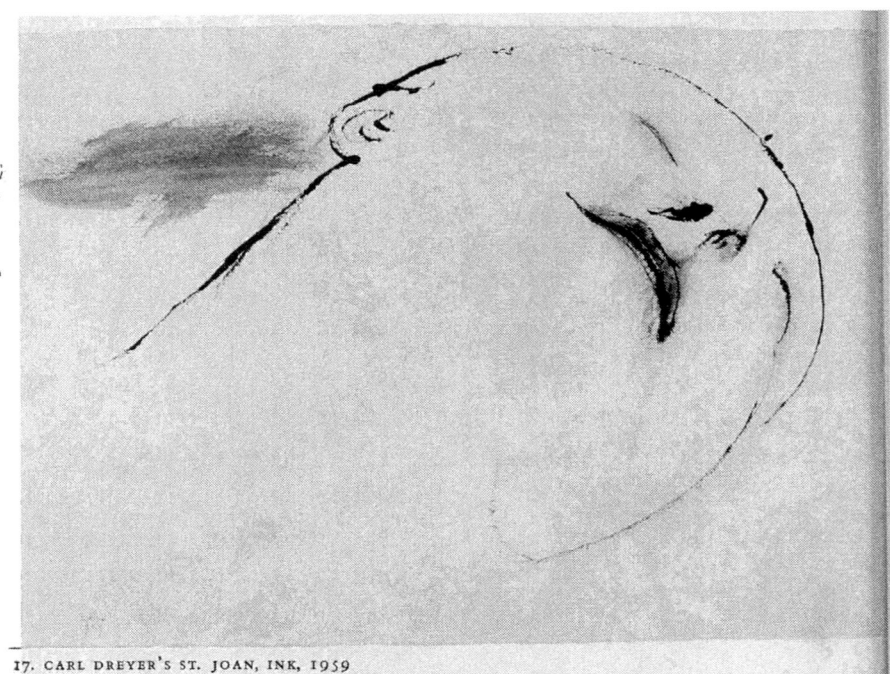

17. CARL DREYER'S ST. JOAN, INK, 1959

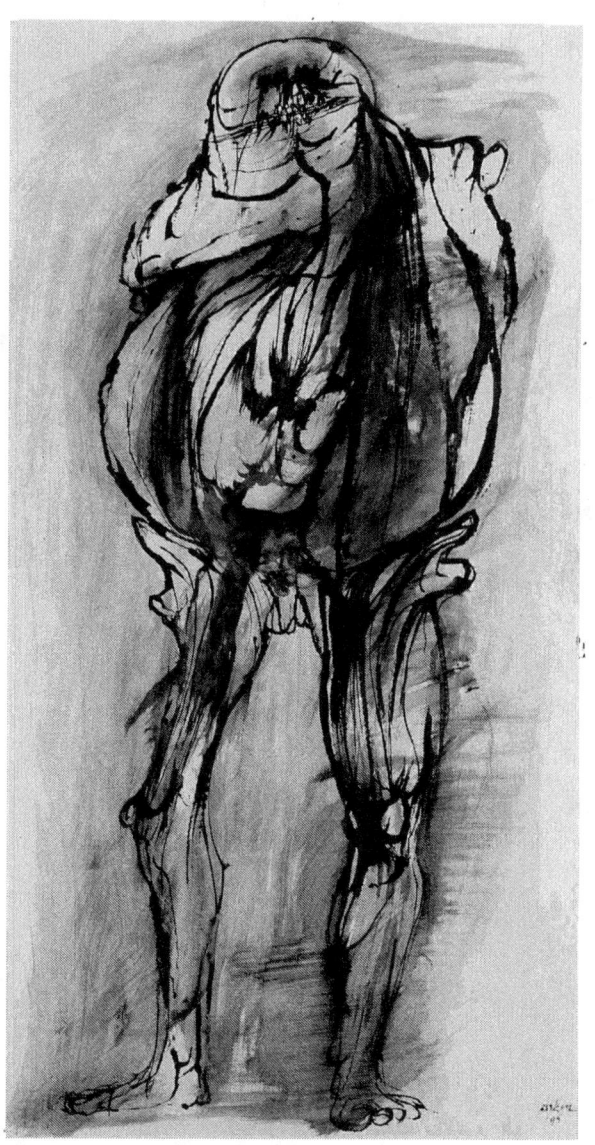

18. GLUTTED DEATH, INK AND WASH, 1959

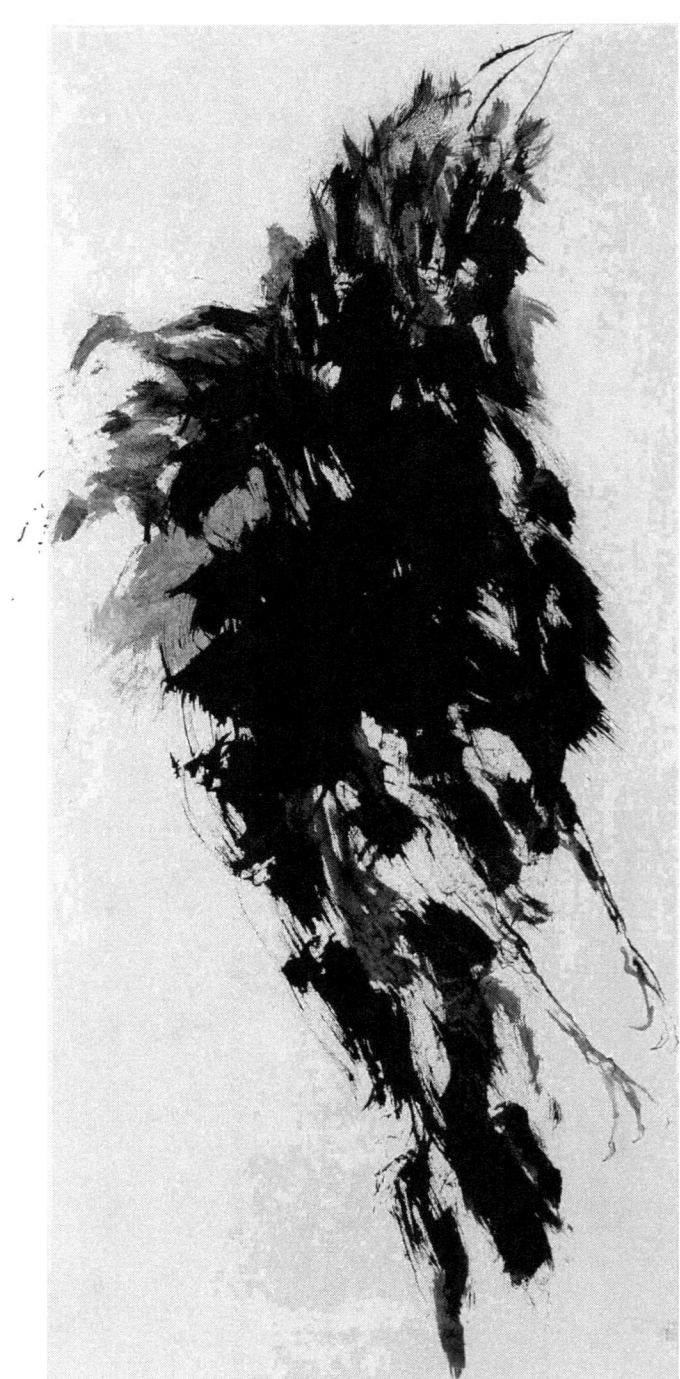

19. DEAD CROW, INK AND WASH, 1959

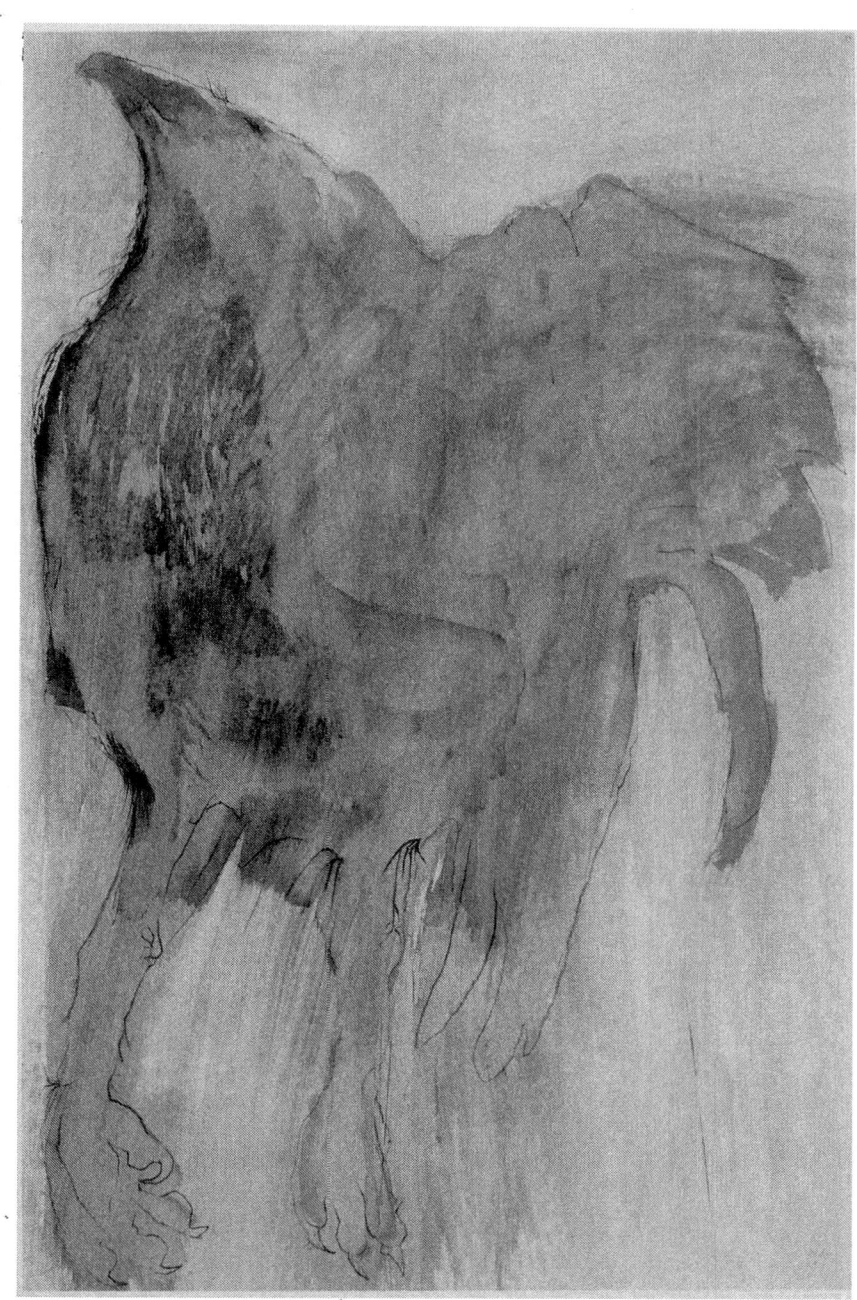

20. SEA BIRD, INK AND WASH, 1960

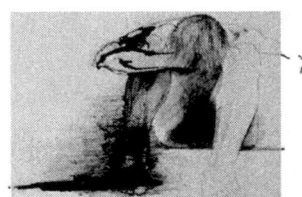

21. STUDY FOR JOB, INK AND WASH, 1961

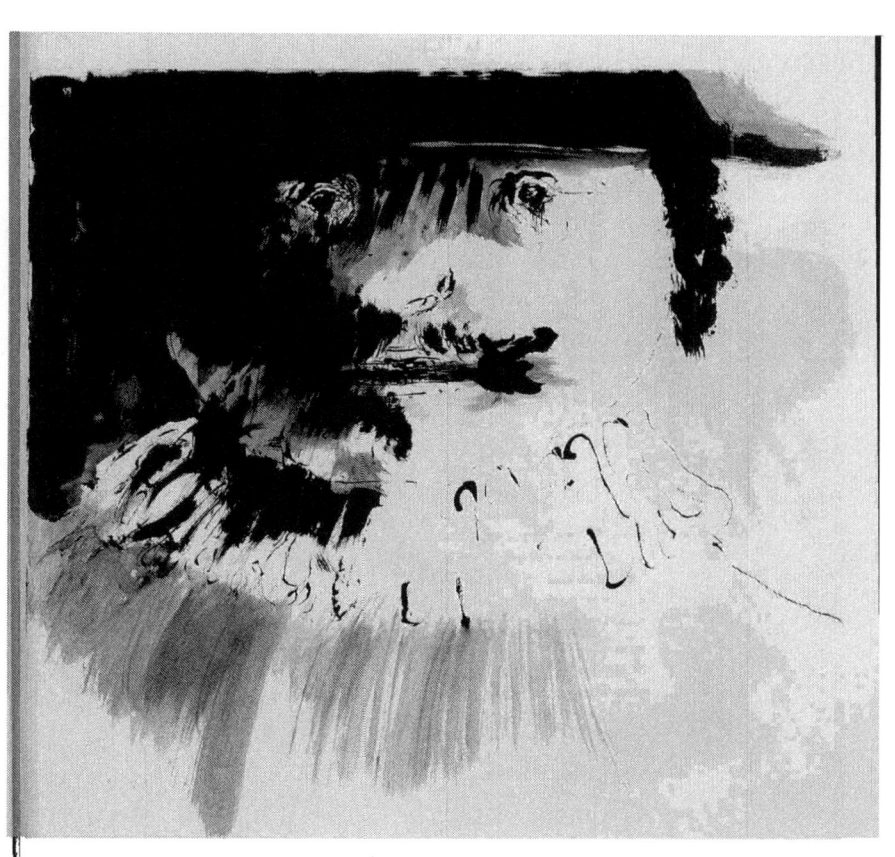

22. REMBRANDT, INK AND WASH, 1961

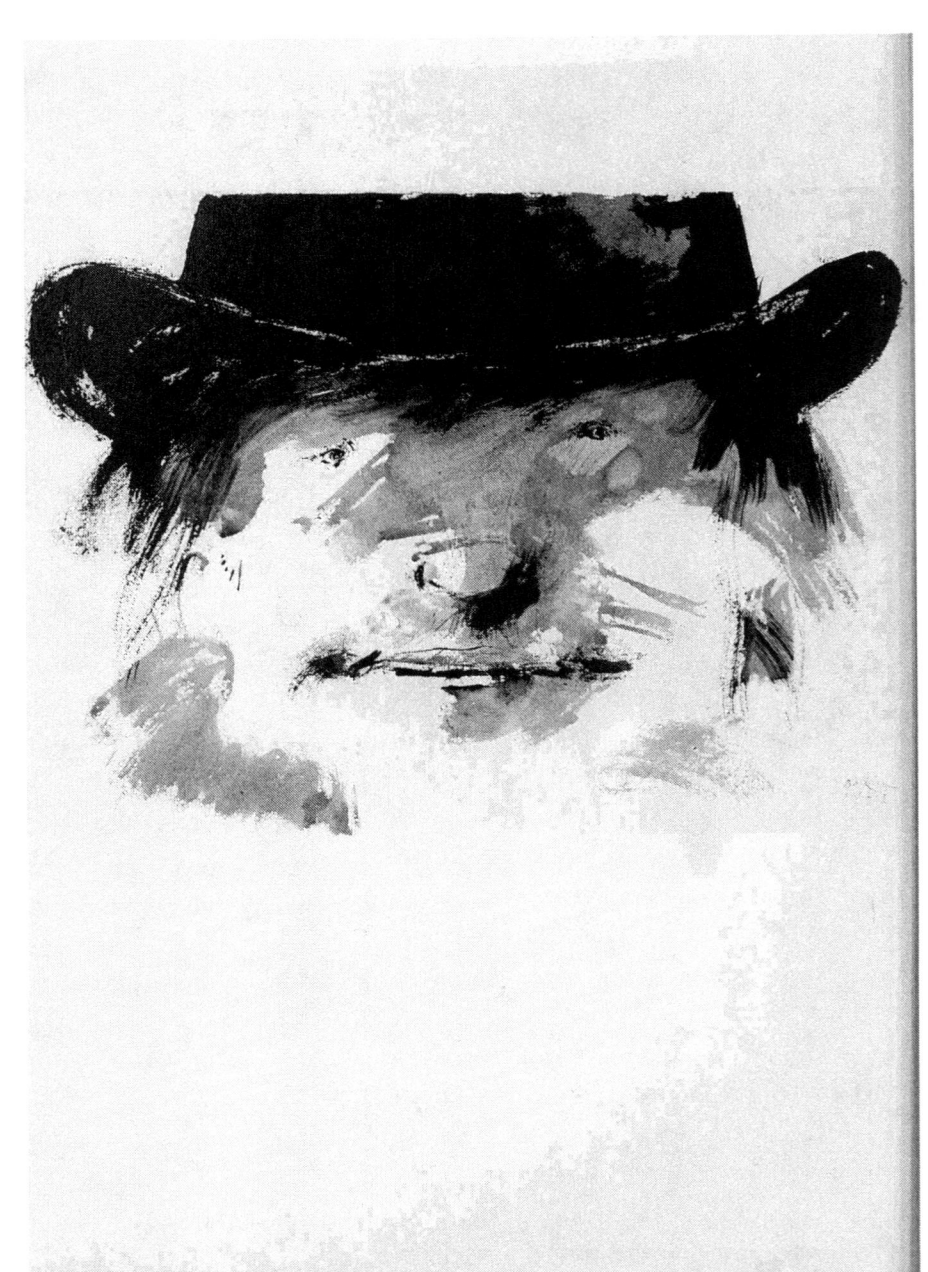

23. DUTCH ARTIST, INK AND WASH, 1961

PRINTS. Among the later etchings of Rembrandt there is one so small it has attracted little attention outside the circle of print lovers. It is called *The Gold-smith* but might more appropriately be called *The Sculptor*. The scene is so intimate that one feels like an intruder in the presence of such absorbing communication between an artist and his almost finished work. Long before I learned that Leonard Baskin knows and loves this etching, I somehow associated it with him. For he is one of that timeless but now very tiny guild of artist-craftsmen to whom Rembrandt paid homage. &➤ Novelty and originality of ideas are justly considered essential criteria of artistic merit, but in our turbulent age of Abstract Expressionism, Non-Art and Anti-Art, they have been extolled beyond all proportion as the *only* valid criteria, sometimes to the point where mere whimsicality and contrived extravagance pose as originality. Baskin has proved that, to be original, one has to be neither a revolutionary nor an iconoclast. He never had need to worry whether or not the critics assigned him a place in the avant-garde, yet there could not be any doubt that his language is contemporary in the best sense of that word. His originality is not contrived, but gradually and organically developed over the years with the maturing of his personality. &➤ In Baskin's work there is never any gap between intention and execution. His superb craftsmanship is not virtuosity per se, but an essential and inseparable part of his mode of expression. Perhaps this is in no small measure due to his profound involvement with book design and illustration, that most exacting branch of art in which poverty of ideas cannot be glossed over by the big gesture. The almost dried-up and forgotten art of wood engraving has been miraculously revitalized by him. The recently published portfolio of his wood engravings from 1948 through 1959 illuminates the long road he has traveled in this field, from the Bewick-like neatness of the earliest to the free and expressive style of the latest. &➤ Yet all these remarks penetrate only to the periphery of Baskin's work; above all, he is a humanist. To understand his work, one has to be as deeply involved with humanity as he is, one has to feel as he does the torment, the anger, the hope, the love and compassion, which never lost their power in thousands of years of human history. It is no wonder, then, that Baskin is deeply involved with poetry and art of the past as well as the present. His erudition in art history is amazing, and as unorthodox as everything else about him. He has explored those remote corners where Altdorfer, the Brothers Hopfer, Buytewech and Seghers, Fuseli and Blake, Bewick, Posada and Bresdin dwell, to name but a few. As an incurable print devotee, I shall never forget the stimulating hours I spent with him browsing through the collection in the Art Institute of Chicago. This erudition, far from making him an eclectic, has helped to develop, I believe, his vital and sensitive style which is finding more and more admirers on both sides of the Atlantic. HAROLD JOACHIM, *Art Institute of Chicago*

PRINTS

1.
BERTOLT BRECHT
Woodcut, 1952, 20¾ × 18¼ ins.
Boris Mirski Gallery
Boston

2.
MAN OF PEACE
Woodcut, 1952, 62 × 31
Boris Mirski Gallery
Boston

3.
THE HYDROGEN MAN
Woodcut, 1954, 62 × 31
Boris Mirski Gallery
Boston

4.
THE HANGED MAN
Woodcut, 1955, 67 × 23
Boris Mirski Gallery
Boston

5.
THE STRABISMIC JEW
Woodcut, 1955, 41½ × 23
Boris Mirski Gallery
Boston

6.
THE POET LAUREATE
Woodcut, 1955, 23 × 48
Boris Mirski Gallery
Boston

7.
TORMENT
Woodcut, 1958, 31 × 23
Bowdoin College Museum of Art
Brunswick, Maine

8.
ANGEL OF DEATH
Woodcut, 1959, 62 × 31
Boris Mirski Gallery
Boston

9.
EVERYMAN
Woodcut, 1960, 83 × 23½
Boris Mirski Gallery
Boston

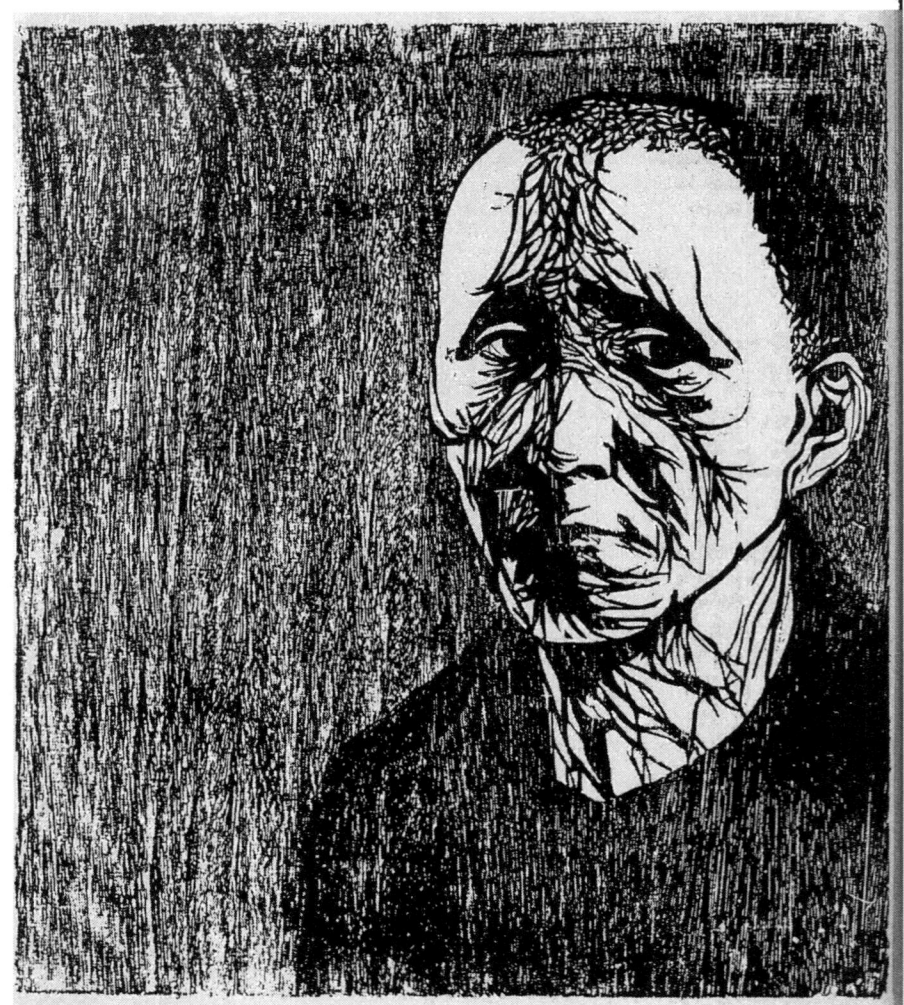

I. BERTOLT BRECHT, WOODCUT, 1952

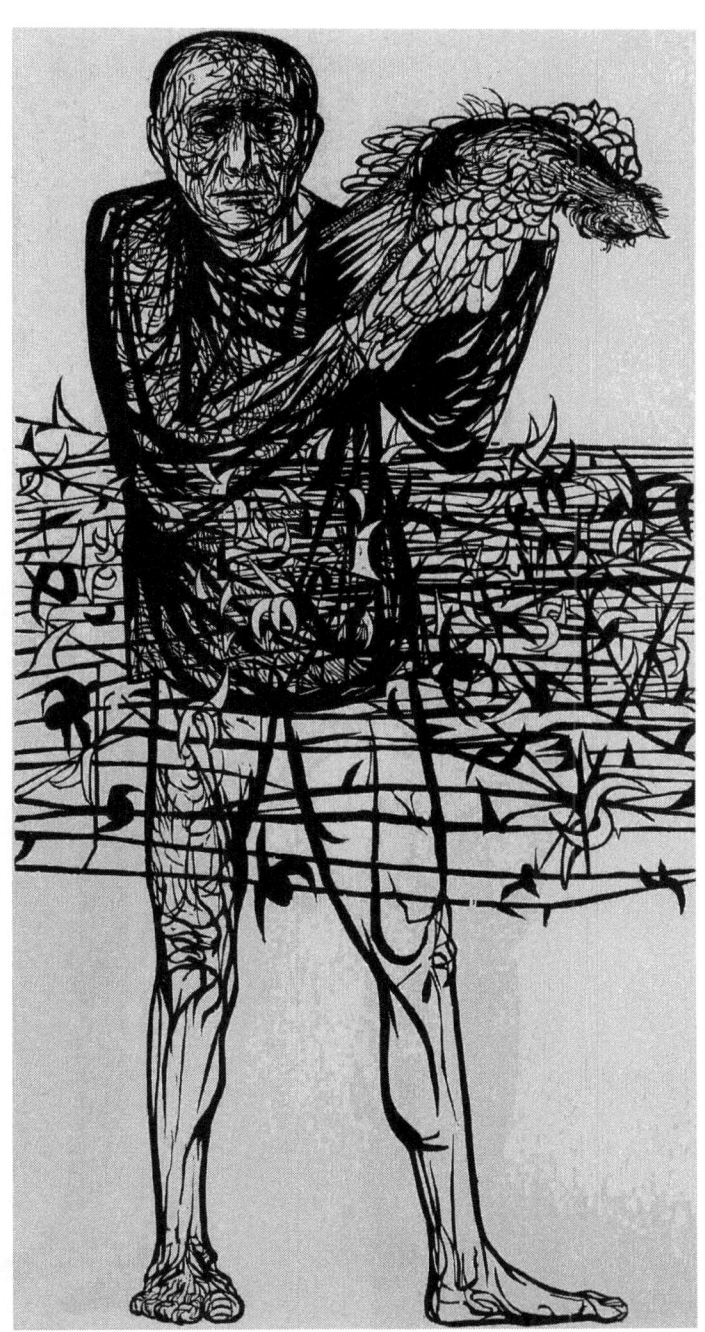

2. MAN OF PEACE, WOODCUT, 1952

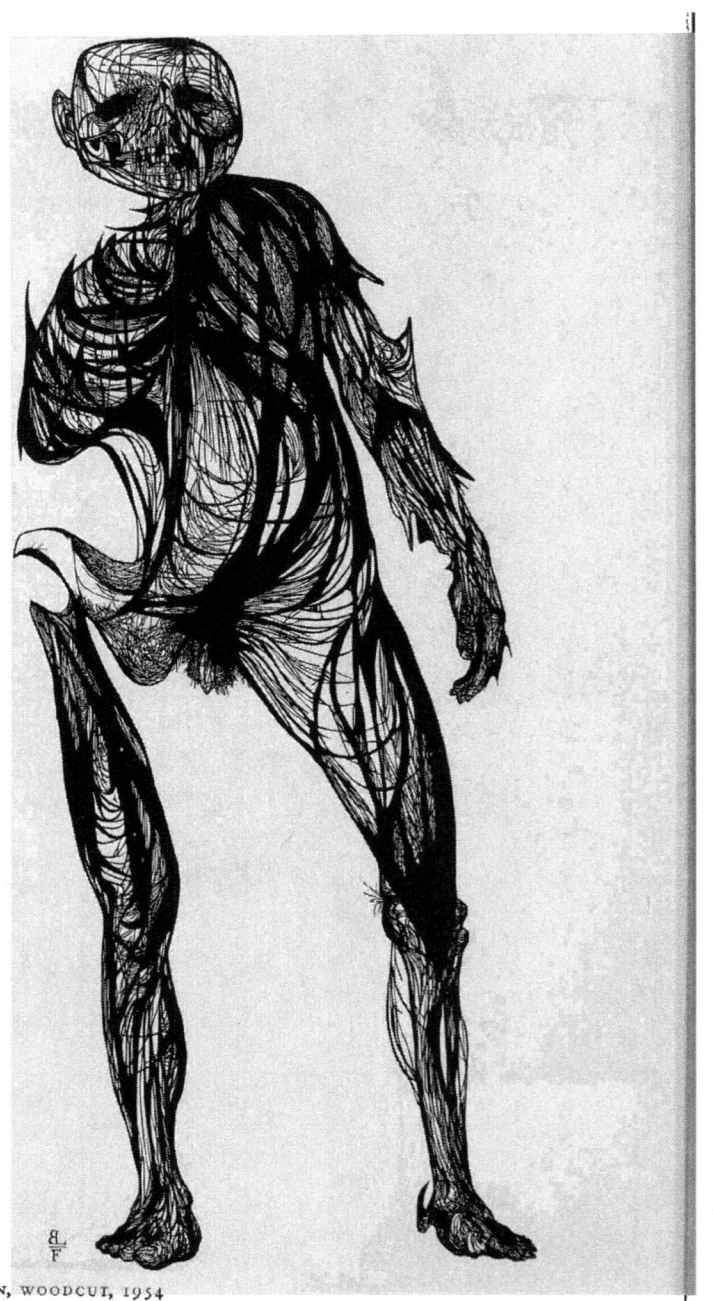

3. THE HYDROGEN MAN, WOODCUT, 1954

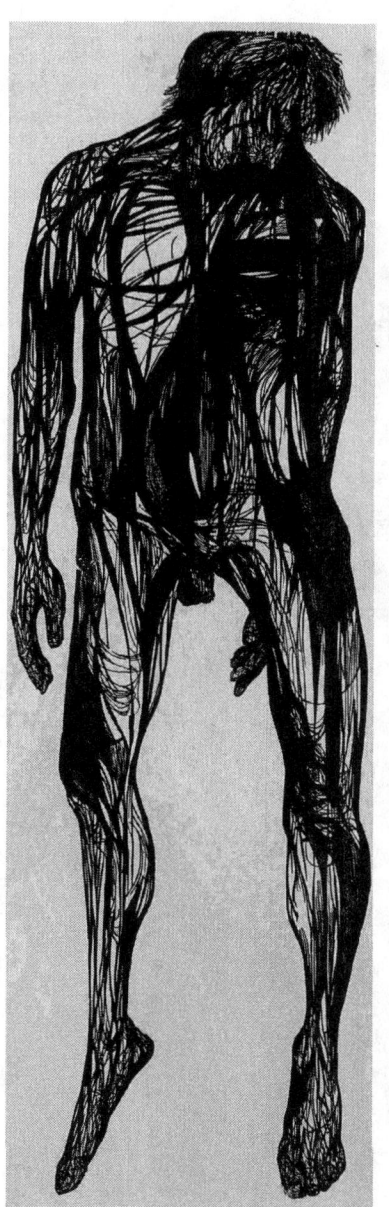

4. THE HANGED MAN, WOODCUT, 1955

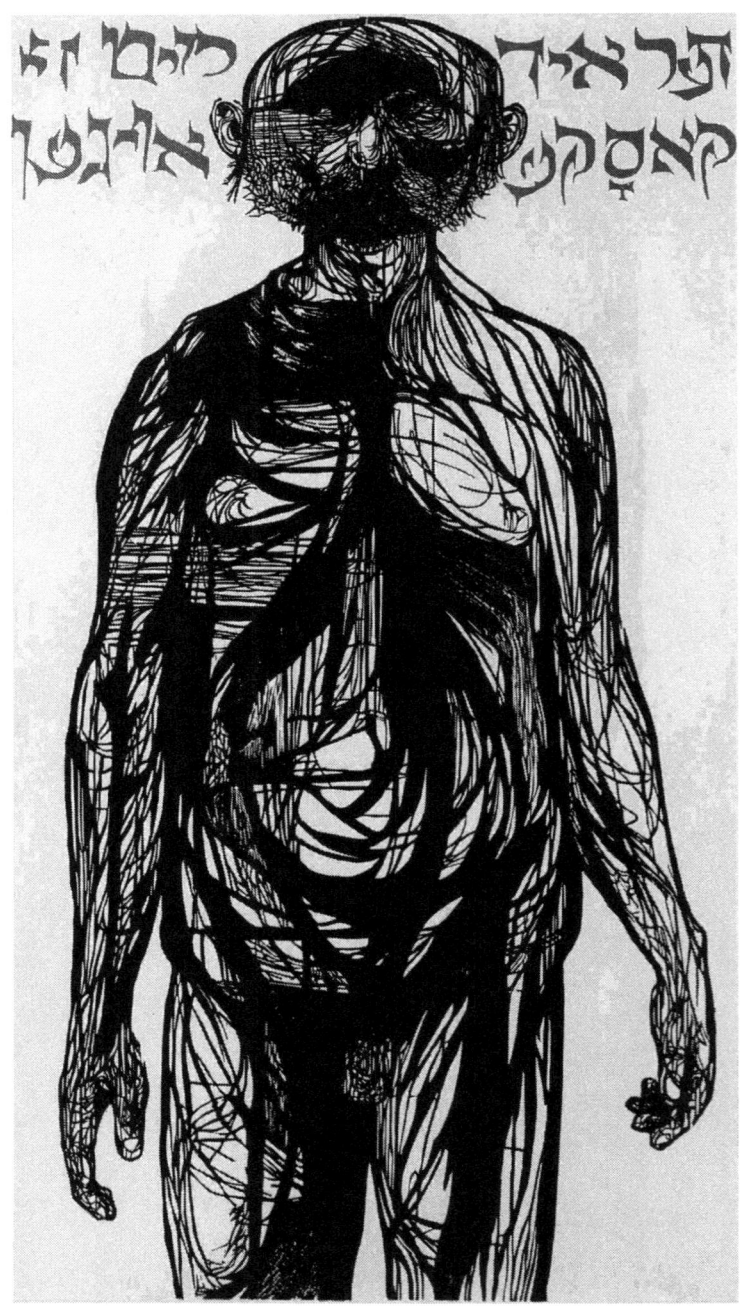

5. THE STRABISMIC JEW, WOODCUT, 1955

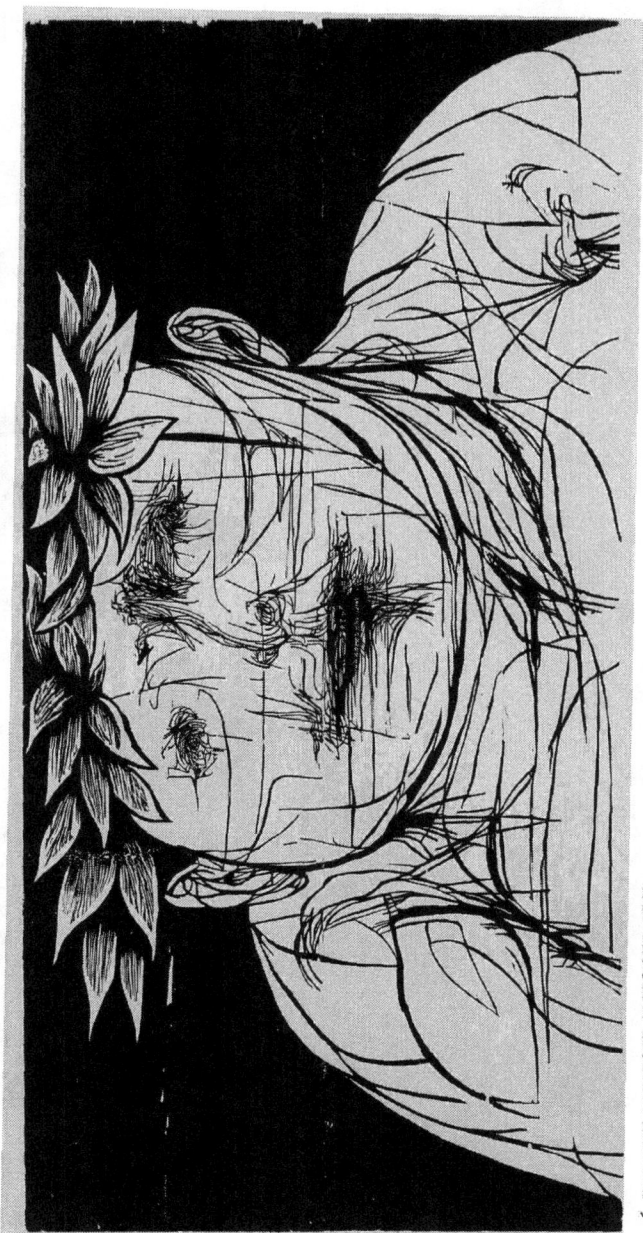

6. THE POET LAUREATE, WOODCUT, 1955

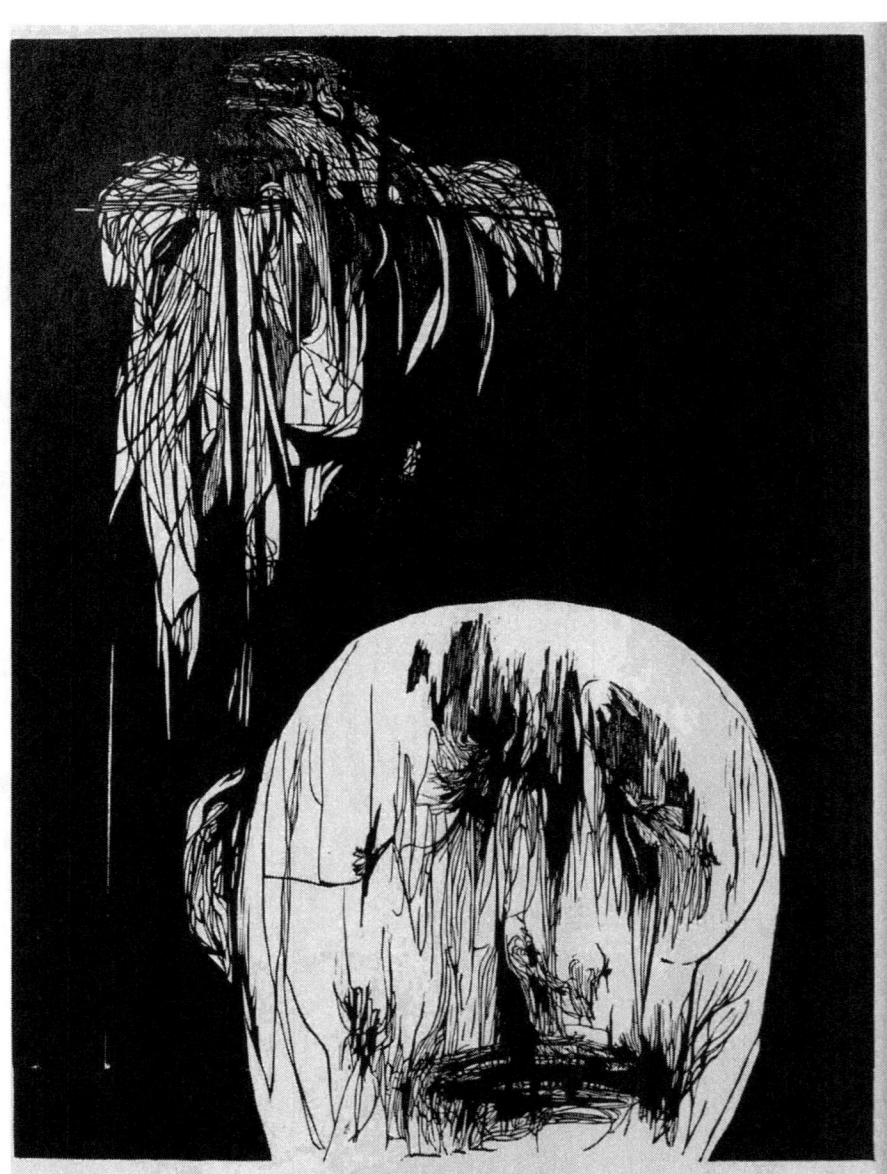

7. TORMENT, WOODCUT, 1958

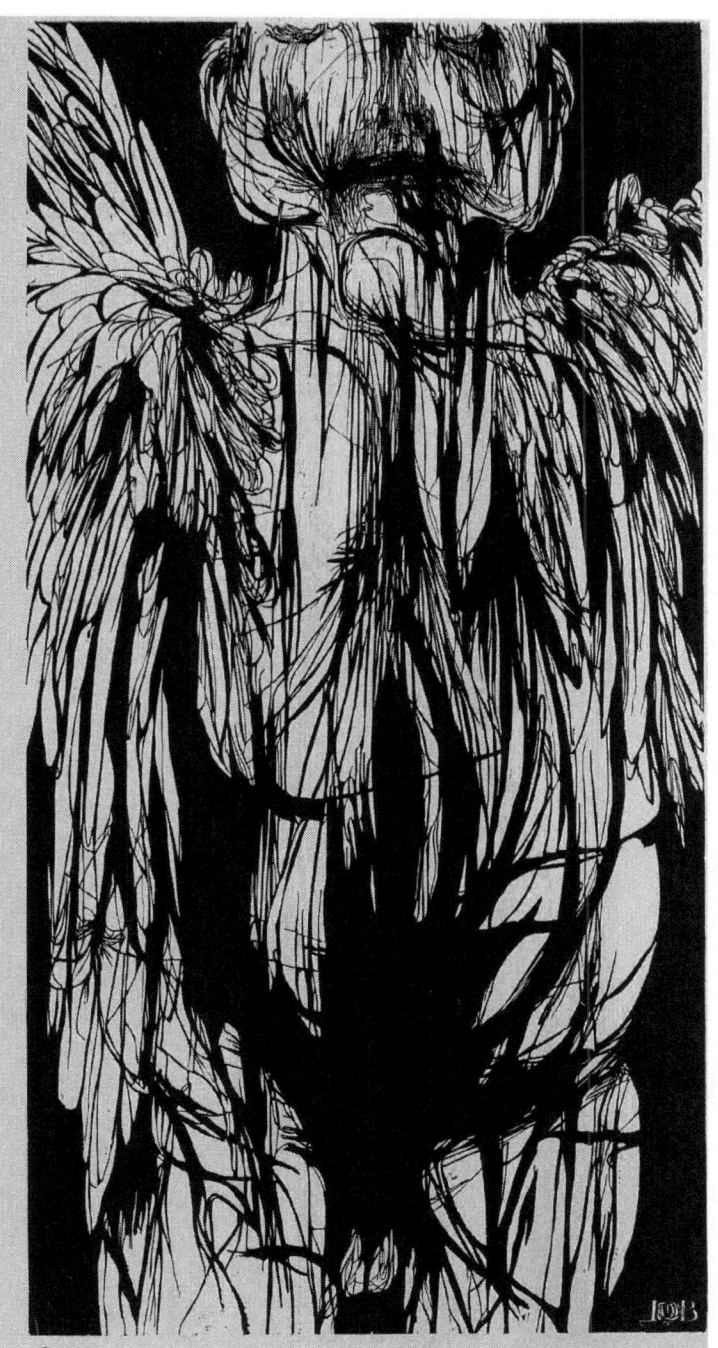

8. ANGEL OF DEATH, WOODCUT, 1959

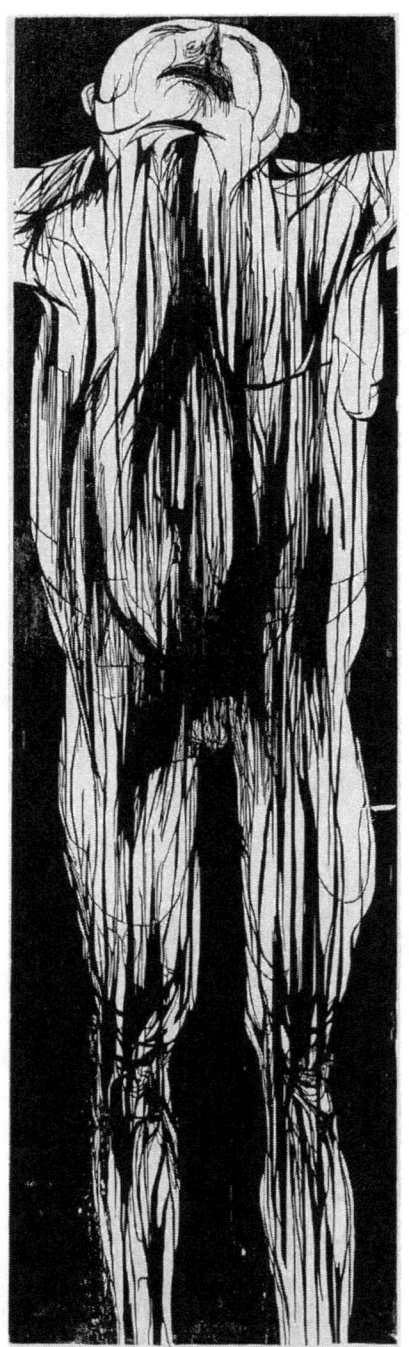

9. EVERYMAN, WOODCUT, 1960

GEHENNA PRESS BOOKS. The beginnings of the Gehenna Press go back twenty years, half its master's lifetime, to the time when he was an art student at Yale. He had written some poems that needed utterance and in Jonathan Edwards Quadrangle he found a printing office with types and a press to the purpose. At the same time he found the name and an unlikely godfather for his imprint, true to the punning and devilish traditions observed by printers for centuries. In the first book of *Paradise Lost* (the author of the *Areopagitica* should have been warier) are lines telling how Moloch took over the pleasant valley of Hinnom, which thence became known as Tophet, 'And black Gehenna call'd, the Type of Hell.' It is quite possible too that in this initial skirmish with typography the young poet and artist had occasion to reflect that here was another place where angels fear to tread. ❧ From such a literary beginning the next turn of the Gehenna Press was toward printmaking interests. The bibliography by Dorothy King records the second appearance of the imprint only after nine years from the date of the incunabulum incunabulorum, *On a Pyre of Withered Roses*, 1942. Number two is a collection in portfolio of prints, mostly from linoleum but also including plank and end-grain wood, titled *A Little Book of Natural History: Engravings by Leonard Baskin*. In ensuing issues from the press as it migrated from Castle Street, Worcester, to Titan's Pier, South Hadley, to Fort Hill, Northampton, the main point of interest continued to be Baskin's woodcuts and wood-engravings. The disavowal of any profit motive 'unless, of course, the reverse is forced upon us' was clearly stated, though naturally in these years the Gehenna Press performed brilliantly as the instrument for making the name and work of Baskin known, for searching out the audience every artist depends upon. ❧ The press was not destined to remain all that private; indeed a certain ambivalence is to be detected as early as 1953 when *The Tunning of Elynour Rummynge* hand set in Artcraft Roman types with plenty of colorful, bold, and unlaced Baskin woodcuts was offered in an edition of 118 copies at $10. This must have done something to breach the strict privacy of the Gehenna Press position. (Whether it was the decisive recommendation to place the proprietor in one of the Heavenly Seven women's colleges as professor of art is still a matter of speculation.) Among other books that featured Baskin wood-engravings and adhered more nearly to the private press character were *Blake and the Youthful Ancients*, 1956; *A Letter from Ernst Barlach*, 1957; and *The Seven Deadly Sins*, 1958. The number of copies respectively was 50, 150 (this was issued as a keepsake), and 300 (plus a second revised printing of the same number). The offer was made to collectors and libraries by means of prospectus. These mailing pieces, sometimes a simple announcement and sometimes a folder enclosing sample pages, are always to be treasured. A case in point is provided by the one for the Blake and friends publication. The paper, like that serving most Gehenna Press printing, is a fine handmade sheet that instantly flatters the eye and intrigues the touch. The cover design is all typographic, a procrustean rectangle built up of one repeated printers' flower to contain the title in red capitals ranged in three lines of even length though uneven letter-spacing. Inside is printed a Blake head by Baskin not included among the eighteen portraits in the book itself. Then there is the text of the announcement to be relished, its lingering over the luxurious names of papers and of exotic special binding materials, and fetching up crisply at the end with a full-bodied, no-nonsense price. And finally, in glowing red, one of those wonderful devices of the press, involving all manner and sizes of pomegranates and owls engraved by the master to go with the Type of Hell. The jewel-like, rubricated, inverted pyramids and other meticulous typographic confections in Gehenna Press printing, along with the conception and laying-out and oversight of much of the work, show where Esther Baskin's fine talents and artistic judgment join those of her husband. In particular the Emily Dickinson *Riddle Poems*, in an edition of 200 copies published in 1957, offered a plat that produced in pure typography under Mrs. Baskin's cultivation what Sir Francis Bacon imagines in *Of Gardens*, another charming nosegay published by the press in 1959. Here are ventures into the almost lost art that, a century and more ago, used to call for the ultimate praiseword of 'dainty' typography. They are refreshing to see and savor. ❧ Another development is to be discerned in Gehenna Press printing. It illuminates a prominent trait in the Baskin character, a singular selfless magnanimity whereby this artist is as eager to publish the work of other artists he admires as he is to publish his own. Instances are the commanding folio of Aubrey Schwartz lithographs, *Predatory Birds*, and *Homage to Redon*, containing ten portrait wood-engravings by George Lockwood. Earlier, he published his great friend Ben Shahn's drawings to illustrate *Thirteen Poems by Wilfred Owen*, to which he played second fiddle by engraving on wood for the book a Shahn portrait of the author. That was in 1956 and though the drawings were reproduced by offset lithography at Meriden there was some apparent struggle in running the letterpress for 400 copies on English handmade at Metcalf Printing & Publishing Company in Northampton. Such a publication was of course far beyond the range of the old Vandercook proof press through which in a simpler era the Baskins had cranked *Elynour Rummynge* page by page. They had need not only of more equipment but also of experienced help in conducting the work through mechanical operations to a controlled product. The first need they supplied through an arrangement with the local commercial plant named; the second by taking Richard Warren into the press organization. The steps were signallized by another series of RW printer's marks and by the announcement that the press stood ready, willing, and able to go to work for anyone. The Gehenna Press at this point proceeded beyond private or even quasi-private press status. It became a personal press offering design, printing, and publishing services to the discriminating public. The output is larger and of better standard. Mr. Baskin never misses a chance of pointing out how much better things look since Harold McGrath took over the presswork. Yet, none of the feeling seems to be lost. Witness *The Wood Engravings of Leonard Baskin*, 1961, of 186 blocks measuring all the way from fifteen-by-sixteen inches down to less than an inch square, printed in a manner to delight the heart of a William Savage. ☜ When he was asked one time about the type faces in use at the press Baskin, looking off in the other direction, said he wasn't 'interested in typography'. Nevertheless when in 1957 the press took on an important commission for the Museum of Modern Art the queer Caslon of the preceding job was laid aside in favor of a smart-looking suit of Perpetua. The Hart Crane *Voyages* came out with Baskin's woodcut and six wood-engravings, some of them printed on exotic tissues or green Moriki, tucked with the brief text into an oblong portfolio. In due course it came up before the jury for the American Institute of Graphic Arts Fifty Books of the Year. The experts considered carefully the colorful swatch of thirteen leaves. It was interesting, undeniably handsome, but was it a book? They decided it was 'contemporary', and they '. . . conceded that the traditionalists have perhaps an easier time, since there are rules and patterns and styles already established for them, while the contemporary designer, striving for mood, must work in what is and should probably remain an unformalized area. . . .' They then selected the Gehenna Press *Voyages* as one of the Fifty of 1957. ☜ Well, 'contemporary designer, striving for mood', may be all right in his place but we shall not find him among the Baskins. They will not be zoned; they will acknowlege no boundaries save those at the limits of their own imagination. For what needs to be done, they place themselves in command of knowledge and skills sufficient to the need. However elusive the necessary materials, they search them out. In the field of book-making 'this limitless trait in the hearts of men' is especially exciting because it plows across old dead-furrows and turns up unexpected areas of fertility in the tired soil. Such fecundity is hardly recognizable in 'striving for mood'. Bottomless resources like these make talk of schemes for teasing out 'creativity' sound hollow and shrill. And anyway Baskin's sights are on some fifteenth-century printing and Carl Rollins's. ☜ There are, Eric Gill said, two typographies, and 'those who use humane methods can never achieve mechanical perfection'. Yet the Gehenna Press has the one and is approaching the other. See—and feel—the forthcoming Gehenna Essays in Art.

RAY NASH, *Dartmouth College*

GEHENNA PRESS BOOKS

1. (King 2) 1952
A Little Book of Natural History
26 linoleum engravings (including title-page vignette and title label on cover),
two wood engravings and one woodcut by Leonard Baskin
30 leaves, 9 × 7, Troya paper
Laid in portfolio
One of 50 copies
Lent by Mr. Baskin

2. (King 7) 1954
A Poem Called The Tunning of Elynour Rummynge, the Famous Ale-Wife of England
Written by John Skelton, Poet Laureate to King Henry VIII
(Text from Dyce's edition of 1843)
Illustrations printed from blocks engraved by Leonard Baskin
23 leaves, 11 ¾ × 7 ¾, Artcraft Roman type, Strathmore Text Paper
Gray-green paper covered boards, with title labels on cover and spine
One of 118 copies
Lent by Mr. Baskin

3. (King 8) 1954 (Second Edition)
Castle Street Dogs
Ten wood engravings by Leonard Baskin
14 leaves, 14 × 9 ½, Troya paper
Issued in sheets
One of 25 copies
Lent Anonymously

4. (King 10) 1956
Blake and the Youthful Ancients
Being Portraits of William Blake and His Followers
With a Biographical Notice by Bennett Schiff
Eighteen wood engravings by Leonard Baskin
24 leaves, 7×6, Goudy Kenntonian type, Mokuroku paper
Half Oasis Niger with paper sides
One of 50 copies
Lent by Mr. Baskin with separate leaves lent Anonymously

5. (King 11) 1956
Thirteen Poems by Wilfred Owen
With drawings by Ben Shahn (Printed by The Meriden Gravure Company)
Portrait of Wilfred Owen engraved by Leonard Baskin from a drawing by
Ben Shahn and printed from the woodblock
18 leaves, 13 ¼ × 10, Ludlow Caslon type, Arnold unbleached paper
Half Oasis Niger with paper sides, in slipcase
One of 400 copies
Lent by Mr. Baskin

6. (King 12) 1957
Voyages. Six Poems from White Buildings by Hart Crane
Six original boxwood engravings; one cherry woodcut on green Moriki paper,
mounted, by Leonard Baskin
13 leaves, 9 ¾ × 11 ¼, Perpetua type, Amalfi paper
Blue paper covers with title label; laid in portfolio with title label
One of 975 copies
(The second book in a series of limited editions published by The Museum of
Modern Art under the direction of Monroe Wheeler)
Lent by Mr. and Mrs. Philip M. Isaacson, Lewiston, Maine

7. (King 13) 1957
Riddle Poems. Emily Dickinson
Designed by Esther Baskin
19 leaves, 6½ × 5¼, Caslon type, Venezia paper
Gray-green paper covered boards, with title labels on cover and spine
One of 200 copies
Lent Anonymously

8. (King 14) 1957
A Letter from Ernst Barlach
Three wood engravings by Leonard Baskin
6 leaves, 6 × 4½, Goudy Kenntonian type, Flemish Laid paper
Orange paper covered boards with title label
One of 150 copies
Lent Anonymously

9. (King 17) 1958
Horned Beetles and Other Insects
34 etchings by Leonard Baskin, printed from the plates by the artist in various
colors on a selection of English, French, Italian, Swiss and Japanese handmade
papers
Full polished morocco, embossed in gold on sides with insect device designed
by the artist
One of 30 copies
Lent by the Department of Printing and Graphic Arts, Harvard College Library,
Cambridge, Massachusetts
Proof sheets lent by Mr. and Mrs. Philip Hofer, Cambridge, Massachusetts

10. (King 19) 1958
The Seven Deadly Sins. Poems by Anthony Hecht
Wood engravings by Leonard Baskin
10 leaves, 8 × 8, Perpetua type, Mokuroku paper
Blue paper wrappers with title label
One of 300 copies
Lent by Mr. Baskin

11. (King 22) 1959
Homage to Redon
Ten portraits Cut and Engraved on Wood by George Lockwood, printed from
the blocks in black and white and color, under the artist's supervision, on a
variety of Japanese handmade papers
With Redon's Essay on Bresdin Lithography and the Nature of Black translated
by Hyman Swetzoff
24 leaves, 11 ¼ × 9 ¼, Caslon type, Millbourn Book Laid paper
Gray Boards with Niger Morocco spine, in slipcase
One of 150 copies
Lent by Mr. Baskin

12. (King 23) 1959
Of Gardens. Francis Bacon
Designed by Esther Baskin
11 leaves, 6 × 4 ¼, Garamond Italic type, Millbourn Book Laid paper
Japanese decorated boards
One of 200 copies
Lent by Mr. Harold Hugo, Meriden, Connecticut

13. (King 24) 1959
Auguries of Innocence. William Blake
Eight wood engravings by Leonard Baskin
8 leaves, 9 ¼ × 5 ¾, Monotype Bembo, Amalfi paper
(Printed for the Print Club of Philadelphia)
One of 250 copies
Lent by Mr. Harold Hugo, Meriden, Connecticut

14. (King 28) 1960
A Letter from Gustave Flaubert
Translated by Francis Steegmuller
One wood engraving by Leonard Baskin
7 leaves, 6 ¼ × 4 ¾, Perpetua type, Mokuroku paper
Gray wrappers
One of 300 copies
Lent Anonymously

15. (King 31) 1961
The Wood Engravings of Leonard Baskin, 1948–1959
186 engravings from the original blocks
74 leaves, 18 × 18 ¼, Herman Zapf's Palatino type, Mokuroku and Umbria paper
Laid in buckram portfolio, enclosed in slipcase with French marbled sides,
Niger Morocco spine tooled in gold and in blind
One of 24 copies
Lent by Mr. Lessing J. Rosenwald, Alverthorpe Gallery, Jenkintown, Pennsylvania

16. (King 32) 1962
Of Garlands and Coronary or Garland Plants. Thomas Browne to John Evelyn Esq.
F. R. S.
6 leaves, 9 ¼ × 6 ⅛, Monotype Bembo, Millbourn Book Laid paper
Green wrappers
500 copies for the Smith College Museum of Art and an overprint of 250 copies
for the Gehenna Press
Lent by Mr. and Mrs. Francis M. O'Brien, Portland, Maine

17. (King 33) 1962
Four Portraits by Francesco Laurana by Ruth Wedgwood Kennedy
Twelve photographs by Clarency Kennedy, reproduced by The Meriden
Gravure Company, printed on Tovil paper
20 leaves, 10 × 7 ¼, Centaur and Arrighi types, Amalfi paper
Boards with vellum spine
One of 500 copies
(The first book in a series of *Gehenna Essays in Art*)
Lent by the Bowdoin College Library, Brunswick, Maine

I am grateful to Miss Dorothy King, Curator of Rare Books at the William Allan
Neilson Library, Smith College, for the use of her bibliography of Gehenna Press
Books, published in the June 1959 issue of *Printing and Graphic Arts*, in preparing my
entries 1–11 and for permitting me to consult the continuation of her bibliography
in typescript for entries 12–17. The King number has been indicated in each case.
I am responsible, however, for the format used in this catalogue and must take the
blame for any descriptive errors in the individual entries. M.S.S.

A LITTLE BOOK
OF NATURAL HISTORY
ENGRAVINGS · · BY
LEONARD BASKIN

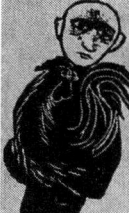

THE GEHENNA PRESS
WORCESTER
1951

1. A LITTLE BOOK
OF NATURAL HISTORY,
1952

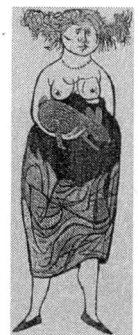

2. A POEM CALLED
THE TUNNING OF ELYNOUR RUMMYNGE,
1954

castle
street
dogs

Wood Engravings By Leonard Baskin

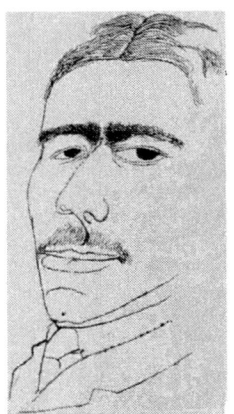

POEMS
WILFRED OWEN

BLAKE AND THE YOUTHFUL ANCIENTS
BEING PORTRAITS OF WILLIAM BLAKE
AND HIS FOLLOWERS ENGRAVED ON
WOOD   BY   LEONARD   BASKIN
AND WITH A BIOGRAPHICAL
NOTICE BY BENNETT SCHIFF
❦❦❦❦❦❦❦❦❦❦❦❦❦❦❦❦
❦❦❦❦❦❦❦❦❦❦❦❦❦❦❦
THE ENTIRE PRINTED
AT THE GEHENNA
PRESS IN NORTH
AMPTON MASS
1 9 5 6
❦❦❦❦
❦❦❦
❦❦
❦

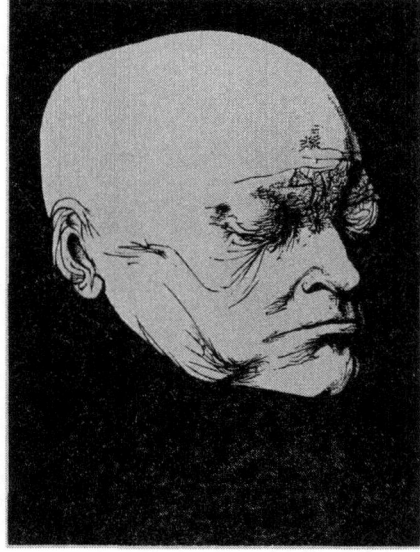

4. BLAKE AND
THE YOUTHFUL ANCIENTS,
1956

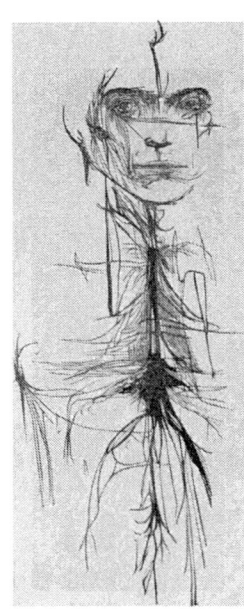

VOYAGES SIX POEMS FROM WHITE BUILDINGS
BY HART CRANE WITH WOOD ENGRAVINGS BY
LEONARD BASKIN PUBLISHED BY THE MUSEUM
OF MODERN ART NEW YORK CITY MCMLVII

6. VOYAGES. SIX POEMS BY HART CRANE, 1957

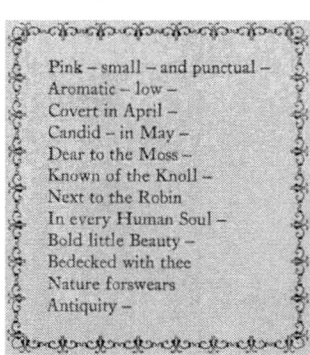

Pink – small – and punctual –
Aromatic – low –
Covert in April –
Candid – in May –
Dear to the Moss –
Known of the Knoll –
Next to the Robin
In every Human Soul –
Bold little Beauty –
Bedecked with thee
Nature forswears
Antiquity –

7. RIDDLE POEMS. EMILY DICKINSON, 1957

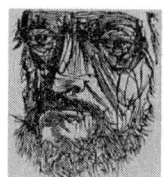

A LETTER FROM ERNST BARLACH

8. A LETTER FROM ERNST BARLACH, 1957

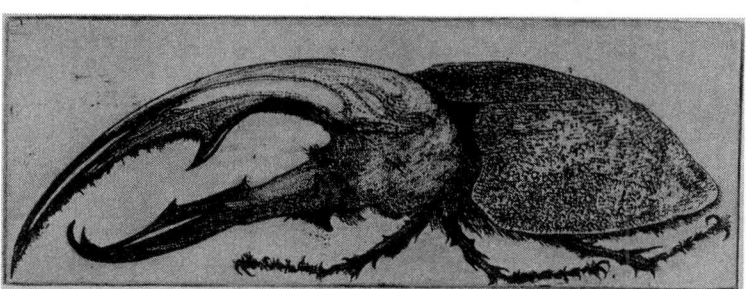

9. HORNED BEETLES AND OTHER INSECTS, 1958

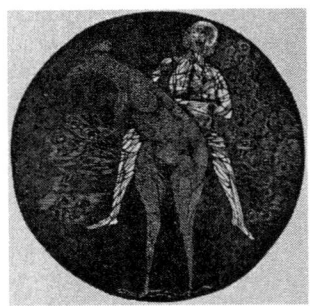

PRIDE

"For me Almighty God Himself has died,"
Said one who formerly rebuked his pride
With, "Father, I am not worthy," and here denied
The Mercy by which each of us is tried.

10. THE SEVEN DEADLY SINS. POEMS BY ANTHONY HECHT, 1958

HOMAGE TO REDON
TEN PORTRAITS
CUT & ENGRAVED ON WOOD
BY
GEORGE LOCKWOOD
WITH
REDON'S ESSAY
ON BRESDIN LITHOGRAPHY AND
THE NATURE OF BLACK
TRANSLATED
BY HYMAN SWETZOFF
THE
GEHENNA PRESS
MCMLIX

11. HOMAGE TO REDON, 1959

divers-coloured earths, that they may lie under the windows of the house on that side on which the garden stands, they be but toys: you may see as good sights many times in tarts. The garden is best to be square, encompassed on all the four sides with a stately arched hedge; the arches to be upon pillars of carpenters' work, of some ten feet high, and six feet broad, and the spaces between of the same dimensions with the breadth of the arch. Over the arches let there be an entire hedge of some four feet high, framed also upon carpenters' work; and upon the upper hedge, over every arch, a little turret, with a belly enough to receive a cage of birds: and over every space between the arches some other little figure, with broad plates of round coloured glass gilt,

for the sun to play upon: but this hedge I intend to be raised upon a bank, not steep, but gently slope, of some six feet, set all with flowers. Also, I understand that this square of the garden should not be the whole breadth of the ground, but to leave on either side ground enough for diversity of side alleys, unto which the two covert alleys of the green may deliver you; but there must be no alleys with hedges at either end of this great enclosure — not at the hither end, for letting your prospect upon this fair hedge from the green — nor at the farther end, for letting your prospect from the hedge through the arches upon the heath.

For the ordering of the ground within the great hedge, I leave it to variety of device, advising, nevertheless, that what-

12. OF GARDENS. FRANCIS BACON, 1959

AUGURIES OF INNOCENCE

To see a World in a Grain of Sand
And a Heaven in a Wild Flower,
Hold Infinity in the palm of your hand
And Eternity in an hour.
A Robin Red breast in a Cage
Puts all Heaven in a Rage.
A dove house fill'd with doves & Pigeons
Shudders Hell thro' all its regions.

A dog starv'd at his Master's Gate
Predicts the ruin of the State.
A Horse misus'd upon the Road
Calls to Heaven for Human blood.
Each outcry of the hunted Hare
A fibre from the Brain does tear.
A Skylark wounded in the wing,
A Cherubim does cease to sing.
The Game Cock clip'd & arm'd for fight
Does the Rising Sun affright.
Every Wolf's & Lion's howl
Raises from Hell a Human Soul.
The wild deer, wand'ring here & there,
Keeps the Human Soul from Care.
The Lamb misus'd breeds Public strife
And yet forgives the Butcher's Knife.
The Bat that flits at close of Eve
Has left the Brain that won't Believe.

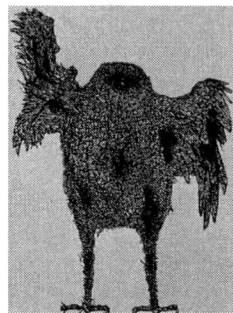

The Owl that calls upon the Night
Speaks the Unbeliever's fright.

13. AUGURIES OF INNOCENCE. WILLIAM BLAKE, 1959

A LETTER FROM GUSTAVE FLAUBERT

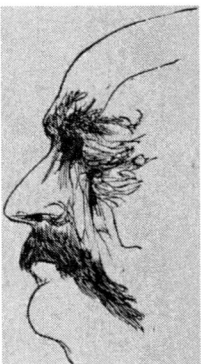

14. A LETTER FROM GUSTAVE FLAUBERT, 1960

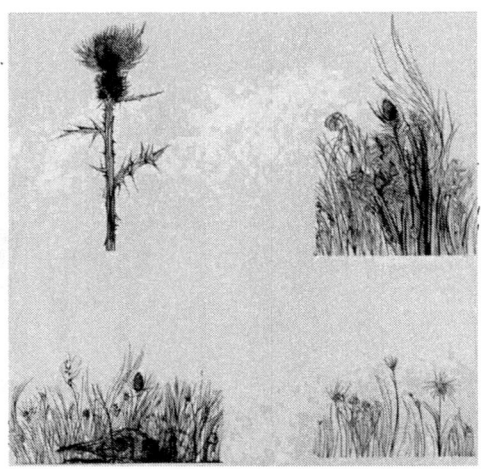

15. THE WOOD ENGRAVINGS OF LEONARD BASKIN, 1948–1959, 1961

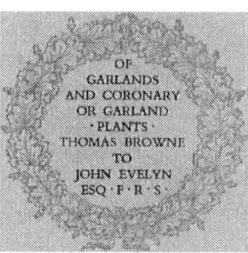

OF
GARLANDS
AND CORONARY
OR GARLAND
· PLANTS ·
THOMAS BROWNE
TO
JOHN EVELYN
ESQ · F · R · S ·

16. OF GARLANDS AND CORONARY OR GARLAND PLANTS, 1962

subsequent history have been snapped by time, the bust would seem to have become a part of the public patrimony of Sicily from this royal source. The Louvre version has been long in France. It was certainly there before the Revolution, when it was confiscated from an *hôtel*. Perhaps, together with much of the Aragonese library, it formed part of the loot brought back to France at the time of the invasion of 1495. ❧ Clearly, these portraits were cherished because of their beauty as works of art and not simply as representations of the hapless Duchess of Milan. These German, French and Italianized Spanish connoisseurs of the mid-1490s evidently found them congenial to their taste. They can hardly have foreseen that the busts would also appeal to a century like ours, so unthinkably distant in time and outlook. For it is an interesting phenomenon that this artist, so peripheral to the Renaissance, always circulating on the outer edge of the Italian world, so limited in his interests in comparison with the willing fabricators of tombs and chapels, so rootless and undisciplined by tradition compared to the sculptors who grew up in a continuous local style—that this maverick Laurana should seem today to be so modern. Although we cannot explain his comings and goings, it is obvious that he was not unappreciated in his own time and that he was always ready enough to respond to the successive artistic and intellectual climates in which he found himself, but he was curiously free from the bondage of the patronage system. If a project failed to interest him, he left its execution to assistants and gave it only desultory attention. If, on the other hand, a project aroused his enthusiasm, he would work on it in solitude, perfecting his own way of realizing his artistic intentions. We may further observe that Laurana was not forgotten in Italy after his death, although he died far away in France. An erudite historian of Neapolitan art wrote in 1524 to an erudite historian of Venetian art giving Francesco credit for the whole such at Naples to which he had contributed only a part. But Laurana was forgotten in Europe, if not in Sicily, during the centuries of the Baroque, the Rococo, the Neoclassical and the Romantic styles. Only the stray appearance on the art market of the oddly unclassifiable busts or masks and the accidental discovery of his name in French, Neapolitan and Sicilian parchments made possible the resurrection of his identity as a sculptor in marble and the collation of this phase of his work with the signed bronze medals. Although little has been written in the past decade or two which adds to our knowledge about Laurana and his work, art historians have continued to grant him an important, if vaguely catalogued,

place in the annals of Italian art. Enthusiasm for his rare productions is now widespread among connoisseurs and practising artists. He has even achieved the eminence of a number of forgeries. ❧ Some of Laurana's latter-day fame can be related to the fabulous resurgence of Piero della Francesca as a painter dear to the twentieth century. Piero, too, was practically forgotten in the intervening years. Montaigne, who reluctantly spent a night in Borgo S. Sepolcro in 1580, wrote in his journal, "There is nothing of artistic interest here," when all he need have done was to step into the Municipio to see the *Resurrection*. But, since the '20s of this century, the abstract properties and geometric organization of Piero's paintings have seemed so much in accord with modern critical criteria and with modern art itself that Piero has outstripped his contemporaries in present-day esteem. Laurana's brief approach to Piero's orbit, his highly original handling of technical and representational problems, his variability of style, his preference for the subjective and the irrational rather than the objective and the rational—even his secretiveness have all combined to rescue Laurana's private language from the limbo of the dead tongues. His art is legible to us today and awakens in us the joy of recognition.

❧ ❧ ❧

17. FOUR PORTRAITS BY FRANCESCO LAURANA BY RUTH WEDGWOOD KENNEDY, 1962

SELECTED BIBLIOGRAPHY

Leonard Baskin, 'Four Drawings, and an Essay on Kollwitz', *The Massachusetts Review*, Vol. 1, No. 1, October 1959, pp. 96–104

Leonard Baskin, 'The Necessity for the Image', *The Atlantic*, Vol. 207, No. 4, April 1961, pp. 73–76

John Canaday, *Embattled Critic, Views on Modern Art*, Farrar, Straus and Cudahy, New York, 1962, pp. 162–165

'Images of Mortality', *Life*, Vol. 42, No. 12, March 25, 1957, pp. 83–84, 87

Brian O'Doherty, 'Leonard Baskin, A Portrait', *Art in America*, Vol. 50, No. 2, Summer 1962, pp. 66–72

Selden Rodman, *Conversations with Artists*, Devin-Adair, New York, 1957, pp. 169–177

Selden Rodman, *The Insiders*, Louisiana State University Press, 1960

Rotterdam, Museum Boymans-van Beuningen, *Leonard Baskin: Sculptuur, Tekeningen, Grafiek*, May 7–July 2, 1961 (Catalogue in Dutch and English of an exhibition under the auspices of the International Council of The Museum of Modern Art, New York, with an essay, 'Leonard Baskin: The Continuance of Tradition' by Peter and Thalia Selz)

São Paulo, VI Bienal Do Museu De Arte Moderna, 1961, *Estados Unidos*. (Catalogue in Portuguese and English of an exhibition under the auspices of the International Council of The Museum of Modern Art, New York, with an essay on Baskin by William S. Lieberman)

Peter Selz, *New Images of Man*, published by The Museum of Modern Art in collaboration with The Baltimore Museum of Art, distributed by Doubleday and Company, Inc., Garden City, New York, 1959, pp. 34–38

'The Monumentalist', *Time*, Vol. 75, No. 2, January 18, 1960, pp. 66–67

Worcester, Massachusetts, Worcester Art Museum, *Leonard Baskin: Sculpture, Drawings, Woodcuts*, November 30, 1956–January 1, 1957 (Exhibition Catalogue)

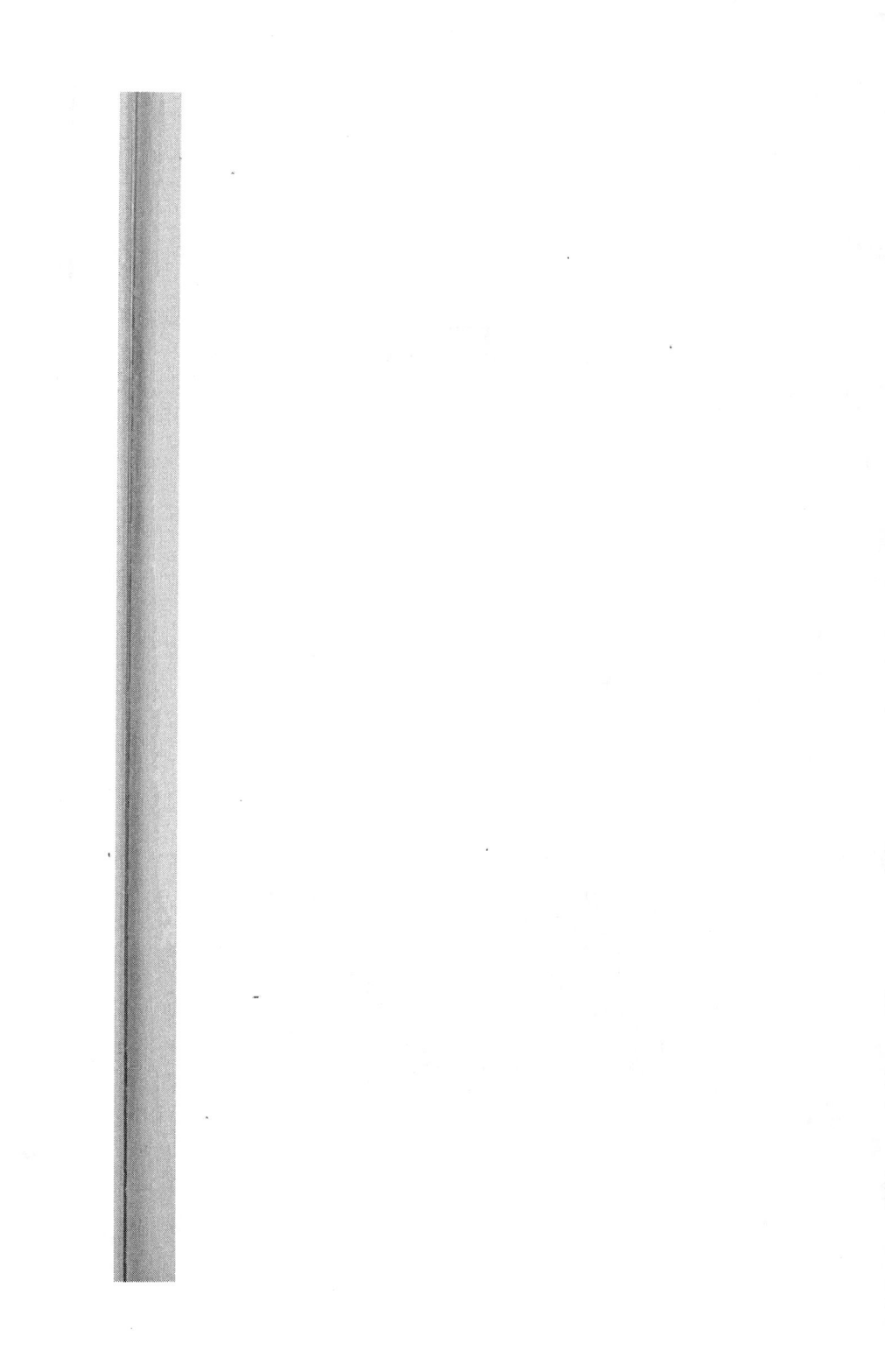

DESIGNED BY LEONARD BASKIN
SET IN TYPE AT THE STINEHOUR
PRESS AND PRINTED AT THE
MERIDEN GRAVURE COMPANY

Photograph credits: SCULPTURE. 5, 6, Oliver Baker Associates, N.Y. 24, Lee Boltin, N. Y. 14, Brenwasser, N. Y. 9, 25, Barney Burstein, Boston. 11, The Detroit Institute of Arts. 8, 10, 12, 13, 16, 22, Otto E. Nelson, N. Y. 34, The Pierce Studio, Brunswick, Me. 30, Nathan Rabin, N. Y. 23, Ron Photo Studio, Yonkers, N. Y. 2, 3, 7, 17, 20, 21, 26, 27, 28, 32, 33, 35, Walter Rosenblum, Long Island City, N. Y. 4, 18, Herbert P. Vose, Wellesley Hills, Mass. 1, Herbert B. Walden, Worcester, Mass. The photograph of DRAWING No. 21 is by Walter Rosenblum and that of PRINT No. 1, by John Brook, Boston. Cover photograph by Nathan Rabin, N. Y. All other photographs were made by The Meriden Gravure Company.

Printed in the USA
CPSIA information can be obtained
at www.ICGtesting.com
LVHW061657031023
759913LV00005B/607